THE LANGUAGE GYM

"Spanish Sentence Builders
A Lexicogrammar approach"
Pre-intermediate - Intermediate

Answer Book

This is the answer booklet for "Spanish Sentence Builders – A Lexicogrammar approach. Pre-intermediate – Intermediate".

It contains answers for all exercises and follows the exact order of the original book.

We hope that you enjoy using it and that your students enjoy working with "Spanish Sentence Builders – A Lexicogrammar approach".

Thanks,

Gianfranco Conti, Dylan Viñales, Jaume Llorens & Verónica Palacín

Imprint: Independently Published
Answer book by Jaume Llorens
Edited by Dylan Viñales, Gianfranco Conti & Verónica Palacín

Table of Contents

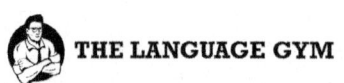 **THE LANGUAGE GYM**

Unit 1: Saying where I live

1. Match

Hay muchos jóvenes – There are many young people

Hay muchas calles peatonales – There are many pedestrian streets

Hay muchos edificios antiguos – There are many old buildings

Hay muchas tiendas – There are many shops

Hay mucho ruido – There is a lot of noise

Hay muchos centros comerciales – There are many shopping centres

Hay muchas instalaciones deportivas – There are many sports facilities

Hay muchos restaurantes buenos – There are many good restaurants

Hay muchas áreas verdes – There are many green spaces

Hay muchos edificios modernos – There are many modern buildings

Hay muchas cosas que hacer – There are many things to do

Hay mucho que ver – There is a lot to see

2. Break the flow

a) Mi ciudad está en el centro de Inglaterra

b) Mi ciudad está en el oeste de Francia

c) En mi ciudad hay muchos bares y discotecas

d) En mi barrio hay mucho que hacer y ver

e) En mi barrio no hay mucha contaminación

f) En mi barrio hay muchas áreas verdes

g) En mi barrio hay muchos centros comerciales

h) En mi barrio hay muchas tiendas que me gustan

3. Missing letters

a) Hay muchas calles peatonales   b) Hay muchos edificios antiguos   c) Hay muchas áreas verdes

d) No hay mucho ruido   e) Hay muchos jóvenes   f) No hay mucha contaminación   g) Hay muchas instalaciones deportivas

4. Translate into English

a) A lot of pollution   b) Many things to do   c) Many shops that I like   d) Many pedestrian streets

e) A lot of noise   f) Many green spaces   g) Many old buildings   h) There is a lot to see

i) There are many sports facilities

5. Complete

a) Hay muchas cosas que **hacer**   b) Hay muchas instalaciones d**eportivas**   c) Hay muchas **áreas** verdes

d) Hay muchos edificios a**ntiguos**   e) Hay muchas **tiendas**   f) Hay mucho **ruido**   g) Hay muchas calles **peatonales**

h) Hay muchos j**óvenes**   i) No hay mucho **tráfico**   j) No hay mucha **contaminación**

6. Faulty translation

a) My *town/**city** is in the **west** of **Germany**   b) I live in a **big** house on the coast

c) –   d) My **neighbourhood** is very big and modern   e) –   f) I **love** my neighbourhood because there is no crime

g) In my neighbourhood there are many **good** shops   h) –

town is not technically a mistake and can be accepted

7. Complete the table

Old buildings – **Edificios antiguos**   Neighbourhood – **Barrio**   **A lot to do** – Mucho que hacer

There is no noise – No hay ruido   Is in the north – **Está en el norte**   **Is in the southeast** – Está en el sureste

Modern buildings – Edificios modernos

8. Complete the table

There is pollution – Hay contaminación   A lot to do – **Mucho que hacer**   **Many things** – muchas cosas

Many good shops – **Muchas tiendas buenas**   **Very clean** – Muy limpio   **In my town/city** – en mi ciudad

In my neighbourhood – **En mi barrio**

THE LANGUAGE GYM

9. Complete the translation

a) There are many **shops** that I like   b) There is a lot to do for **young people**   c) There are a lot of **green spaces**

d) One can **eat** well   e) It is a **safe** neighbourhood   f) There is a lot of **pollution**   g) There isn't much **noise**

10. Translate into English

a) In my city there is a lot to do for young people

b) In my neighbourhood there are many good bars and restaurants

c) I love my neighbourhood because there are many sports facilities

d) The best thing about my neighbourhood is that it is safe

e) The best thing about my neighbourhood is that it is very clean and quiet

f) In my neighbourhood there are many malls with many good shops

g) In my neighbourhood there is a lot to do for children

h) The worst thing about my city is the pollution

11. Correct the grammar/spelling errors

a) Muchos edificios antiguo**s**   b) Hay mucho **que** hacer   c) M**e** encanta mi barrio   d) Hay mucha**s** tiendas buen**as**

e) Est**á** en el norte de Alemania   f) Hay muchos j**ó**venes   g) Hay much**a** contaminaci**ó**n

h) Hay mucho que hacer para los j**ó**venes y los ni**ñ**os

12. Sentence puzzle

a) En mi barrio hay mucho que hacer   b) Mi ciudad está en el norte de Inglaterra

c) En mi calle hay muchas tiendas buenas   d) Vivo en un barrio muy grande y moderno

e) Mi ciudad está en el sur de España   f) En mi calle hay muchos edificios históricos

13. Match

Antiguo – Old   **Moderno** – Modern   **Limpio** – Clean   **Sucio** – Dirty   **Feo** – Ugly   **Bonito** – Beautiful

Tranquilo – Quiet   **Ruidoso** – Noisy   **Seguro** – Safe   **Peligroso** – Dangerous

14. Multiple choice

Tiendas buenas ; Edificios antiguos ; Mucho que hacer ; Mucho que ver ; Una calle sucia ; Una ciudad fea ;
Hay muchas cosas ; Tiendas caras ; Está en el sur

15. Complete with the correct option

a) En mi ciudad **hay** mucho que ver y hacer   b) Mi ciudad **está** en el norte

c) En mi **calle** hay muchos edificios antiguos   d) En mi barrio hay muchas **tiendas** bonitas

e) Me **encanta** mi barrio porque no hay ruido   f) Me gusta mucho la **gente** de mi barrio

g) Mi barrio es un **lugar** seguro   h) En mi ciudad hay mucho que hacer para los **jóvenes**

16. Match

Mucho que hacer – A lot to do   **En mi barrio** – In my neighbourhood   **En mi ciudad** – In my town

Edificios antiguos – Old buildings   **En el norte** – In the north   **La gente** – The people

Para los jóvenes – For young people   **Muchas tiendas** – Many shops   **Áreas verdes** – Green spaces

En mi calle – In my street   **Muchas cosas** – Many things

17. Spot the intruders

a) Me gusta **mucho** la gente de mi barrio   b) En mi calle hay muchas tiendas **buenas**

c) Mi ciudad está en el norte **del país**   d) Lo peor de mi barrio es la contaminación **del aire**

e) En mi barrio **siempre** se puede hacer muchos deportes al aire libre

f) En mi barrio **no** hay mucho que hacer para los jóvenes   g) Mi barrio está en las afueras **de la ciudad**

h) Me encanta mi barrio porque hay muchos edificios históricos **muy bonitos**   i) Mi barrio es **demasiado** ruidoso

18. Find in the text

a) Soy de   b) Está situada   c) Un barrio muy bonito   d) Muchísimos edificios   e) Instalaciones deportivas

f) Hay mucho que hacer   g) El (barrio) más animado   h) Muchas tiendas buenas   i) Lo que no me gusta   j) Mucho ruido

 **THE LANGUAGE GYM**

2

19. Complete the translation of Ian's text

East ; coast ; ugly ; outskirts ; dirty ; sports facilities ; shops ; young people ; crime ; go out ; furthermore/besides ; factories ; pollution ; near/close to ; noise ; worst

20. Answer the questions on Ian's text

a) Dieciséis años   b) En Valencia   c) Es de Reading   d) En las afueras de la ciudad   e) Sucios y feos   f) No

g) No es seguro, porque hay mucho crimen   h) Porque hay muchas fábricas

i) Porque el edificio está muy cerca del aeropuerto   j) Lo peor de todo es que hay mucho ruido

21. Find in the text

a) Por el trabajo de mi padre   b) Está situada   c) Bonito   d) Así que hay   e) Ruido   f) Siempre hay atascos

g) Eso es lo peor de todo   h) Para los jóvenes   i) Es muy animado   j) Calles peatonales   k) Al aire libre

l) Que están abiertas hasta las seis de la mañana   m) Muchas tiendas bonitas   n) La gente de mi barrio

o) Demasiados turistas   p) Es bastante seguro   q) En las calles

22. Comprehension questions

a) On the outskirts of the city   b) Swimming pools and sports centres   c) Cinema, bowling alley, skating ring, good shops

d) There isn't any   e) Botanical garden, museum, swimming pool, mall, park   f) Jogging, rides the bike, walks the dog

g) Polite, calm, helpful   h) There are many green spaces, she likes nature

23. Complete the sentences

a) gente / simpática   b) barrio / contaminación   c) hay / fábricas   d) muchos / ruido

e) ciudad / áreas verdes   f) calle / tiendas   g) mi / lugar / seguro   h) casa / parque / bici / perro

24. Translate into English

a) factories   b) there is/are   c) shops   d) neighbourhood   e) city   f) one can   g) facilities

h) furthermore/besides   i) street   j) park   k) near   l) it is safe

25. Find in the wordsearch

Good shops – **Tiendas buenas**   Near my house – **Cerca de mi casa**

There are – **Hay**   There is pollution – **Hay contaminación**

The best thing – **Lo mejor**   The people – **la gente**   In my street – **En mi calle**

The worst thing – **Lo peor**   In my neighbourhood – **En mi barrio**

26. Complete with suitable words (accept any other correct answers)

a) ciudad   b) afueras   c) peligroso   d) hay / buenas   e) mucho / seguro

f) contaminación   g) tienda   h) sucio, feo / gusta

27. Form logical phrases

Vivo en el sur de España ; Hay un polideportivo grande ; La gente es muy simpática y servicial ;

Mi ciudad está en el norte de España ; Me gusta mucho mi barrio ; Hay tiendas buenas ; Lo peor de mi barrio es el tráfico ;

En mi barrio hay muchas fábricas ; Mi edificio es feo y está mal cuidado ; En mi ciudad hay mucha contaminación

28. Guided translation

a) En mi barrio hay mucho tráfico

b) No me gusta mi barrio porque está sucio y es peligroso

c) En mi calle hay muchas tiendas buenas

d) Mi ciudad está en el norte de Inglaterra

e) Lo peor de mi barrio es la contaminación

f) En mi ciudad hay mucho que hacer para los jóvenes

g) Cerca de mi casa hay un parque y una piscina

h) Lo mejor de mi barrio es que es seguro

i) Por lo general, la gente de mi barrio es muy educada

j) Cerca de mi casa hay un jardín botánico

29. Spot the missing word

a) En **mi** barrio hay mucha contaminación   b) En mi ciudad **hay** muchas áreas verdes c) Por lo general, en mi barrio la gente **es** muy simpática   d) En mi calle **hay** muchas tiendas buenas   e) Vivo en **un** edificio muy antiguo y feo

f) Vivo en **un** barrio histórico   g) Lo peor **de** mi barrio es el ruido   h) Vivo muy cerca **del** aeropuerto

i) Cerca de mi casa hay un parque muy bonito donde monto **en** bici   j) Mi barrio **es** muy feo

30. Tangled translation

a) Mi ciudad **está** el sur **de España**   b) Vivo **en una** ciudad en el **norte** de **Francia**   c) Mi **ciudad** se llama Niza. Está **cerca** de Italia   d) Me encanta **mi** ciudad **porque** es **muy** hermosa   e) Cerca de mi **casa** hay un **centro comercial**

f) Mi **barrio** está en las **afueras de** Cádiz   g) Mi barrio **es** muy **grande** y **moderno**

h) Hay muchas **áreas** verdes e instalaciones deportivas como **piscinas** y un **gimnasio**

i) No **hay** muchas tiendas **pero** hay un centro comercial no muy **lejos** de mi **casa**

j) En mi **calle** hay un parque muy **grande** donde monto en **bici** y paseo al **perro**

k) Lo **mejor de** mi barrio es **que** la gente **es** simpática

31. Translate into Spanish

a) Vivo en un pueblo/una ciudad   b) Mi barrio es   c) Cerca de mi casa   d) Áreas verdes   e) Hay un centro comercial

f) En mi calle   g) No lejos de   h) Paseo al perro i) Monto en bici   j) En el norte de España

k) En las afueras l) Me encanta mi barrio   m) Lo mejor   n) Mucho que hacer para los jóvenes

32. Translate into Spanish

Vivo en un pueblo/una ciudad en el norte de España. Mi barrio está en las afueras de la ciudad. Mi barrio es grande y moderno. Hay muchas áreas verdes e instalaciones deportivas. No hay muchas tiendas, pero hay un centro comercial cerca de mi casa. En mi calle hay un gimnasio, un supermercado pequeño y un bar. Cerca de mi casa hay un parque grande donde monto en bici y paseo a mi perro. Lo mejor de mi barrio es que la gente es simpática y educada. Lo peor es que no hay mucho que hacer para los jóvenes.

33. Complete the sentences creatively

Accept any grammatically correct sentence. Less experienced students can adapt existing answers from the unit.

34. Write a sentence for each of the following words As above.

35. Spot and correct the spelling/grammar mistakes

a) Mi barrio **está** en la**s** afueras de la ciudad   b) Cerca de mi casa **hay** una tienda de deporte

c) **Lo** peor de mi barrio es la contaminación   d) Lo mejor de mi barrio es **el** ruido   e) ¿Dónde está **tu** barrio?

f) La gente de mi barrio **es** simpá**tica**   g) Mi barrio **es** muy grande y moderno

36. Write a paragraph in Spanish about Marta in the first person singular (I) and one about Roberto in the third (he)

Marta Mi ciudad está en el norte de España. Mi barrio está en el centro de la ciudad. Hay muchas instalaciones deportivas dos polideportivos, un club de tenis y tres gimnasios. En mi barrio hay dos parques grandes, pero también hay mucha contaminación. Para los jóvenes hay muchos bares, discotecas y conciertos. Lo mejor de mi barrio es que es seguro, y lo peor es que hay muchos turistas y el ruido. La gente de mi barrio es muy simpática y educada.

Roberto Su ciudad está en el sur de Argentina. Su barrio está en las afueras de la ciudad. Hay una piscina, un estadio y un polideportivo, y solo hay un parque pequeño. No hay contaminación, pero hay un poco de ruido. No hay mucho que hacer para los jóvenes, porque solo hay un centro comercial y el parque. Lo mejor de su barrio es el estadio, y lo peor es el crimen. La gente de su barrio es antipática y maleducada.

Question Skills Unit 1

1. Split questions ¿**Dónde** vives? / ¿**En qué parte del país** está tu ciudad? / ¿**Qué hay** para los jóvenes?
¿**Qué sitios** turísticos hay? / **Describe** tu ciudad / ¿**Qué es lo** mejor de tu ciudad? / ¿**Qué es lo peor** de tu ciudad?
¿**Te gusta** tu barrio? / ¿**Cómo son las** tiendas de tu barrio? / ¿**Por qué** no te gusta?

2. Find and write in the missing words

a) Describe **tu** ciudad

b) ¿Por qué no **te** gusta tu barrio?

c) ¿En qué parte de tu ciudad **está** tu barrio?

d) ¿Qué hay para **los** jóvenes en tu ciudad?

e) ¿Qué sitios turísticos **hay** en tu ciudad?

f) ¿Cómo son las tiendas **de** tu barrio?

g) ¿Qué es **lo** peor de tu ciudad?

h) ¿Qué **es** lo mejor de tu ciudad?

i) ¿Qué se puede **hacer** en tu barrio?

3. Match questions and answers

¿**Dónde está situada tu ciudad?**	– En el sur de Alemania
¿**Dónde está tu barrio?**	– En las afueras de la ciudad
¿**Cómo se llama tu barrio?**	– Se llama Bogenhausen
¿**Qué hay en tu barrio para los jóvenes?**	– Hay parques bonitos y un centro comercial
¿**Cómo es la vida nocturna?**	– ¡Es fenomenal! Hay muchas discotecas
¿**Qué es lo peor de tu barrio?**	– La contaminación, por supuesto
¿**Qué es lo mejor de tu barrio?**	– La tranquilidad
¿**Hay muchas áreas verdes?**	– Sí. Hay muchos parques
¿**Te gusta tu edificio?**	– No, porque es feo y antiguo
¿**Cómo te llamas?**	– Me llamo Hans
¿**Cuántos años tienes?**	– Tengo diecisiete años
¿**Qué haces en tu tiempo libre?**	– Monto en bici en el parque cerca de mi casa
¿**Cómo es la gente de tu barrio?**	– Es muy simpática y educada

4. Guided translation

a) ¿Por qué no te gusta tu pueblo?   b) ¿Hay muchas áreas verdes?   c) ¿Te gusta tu edificio?
d) ¿Dónde está tu barrio?   e) ¿Cómo es la vida nocturna?   f) ¿Qué sitios turísticos hay?
g) ¿Dónde está situada la ciudad?   h) ¿Qué es lo peor de tu ciudad?

5. Translate a) ¿Por qué no te gusta...?   b) ¿Dónde está (situado) León?   c) ¿Qué hay en...?   d) ¿Cómo es...?
e) ¿En qué parte...?   f) ¿Qué es lo peor?   g) ¿Qué es lo mejor?   h) ¿Hay...?   i) ¿Qué tiendas hay?

6. Answer the following questions in your own words
Accept any grammatically correct sentence. Less experienced students can adapt existing answers from the unit.

THE LANGUAGE GYM

Unit 2: Saying what I can do in my neighbourhood

1. Match

Se puede hacer deporte – One can do sport

Se puede ir al estadio – One can go to the stadium

Se puede ir al cine – One can go to the cinema

Se puede hacer footing – One can go jogging

Se puede ir de compras – One can go shopping

Se puede ir de paseo – One can go for a walk

Se puede ir a la piscina – One can go to the swimming pool

Se puede ir de marcha – One can go clubbing

Se puede ir a la bolera – One can go to the bowling alley

Se puede ver conciertos – One can see concerts

Se puede ver partidos de fútbol – One can see football matches

Se puede visitar galerías de arte – One can visit art galleries

2. Complete with *hacer, ir, ver* o *visitar*

a) Se puede **hacer** deporte   b) Se puede **hacer** turismo   c) Se puede **hacer** footing   d) Se puede **ir** al estadio

e) Se puede **visitar** castillos   f) No se puede **ir** de marcha   g) Se puede **ir** de paseo   h) Se puede **ver** conciertos

3. Break the flow

a) Se pueden visitar galerías de arte en el casco antiguo

b) Se puede ir de paseo en la playa

c) Se puede hacer footing en el parque

d) Se pueden ver conciertos en el estadio

e) Se pueden ver partidos de fútbol en el estadio

f) Se pueden visitar castillos en el casco antiguo

g) Se puede comprar ropa de marca en la calle peatonal

h) Se puede hacer deporte en el centro polideportivo

4. Sentence puzzle

a) Se pueden ver partidos de fútbol   b) Se puede ir de paseo en el parque   c) Se puede ir de marcha en el centro

d) Se puede visitar un castillo en el casco antiguo   e) Se puede hacer deporte en el polideportivo

5. Translate into English

a) One can go for a walk   b) One can go clubbing   c) One can go to the swimming pool   d) One can go shopping

e) One can buy branded/designer clothes   f) One can ride the bike   g) One can go to the skating rink

h) One can see matches   i) One can go jogging in the park

6. Match actions and places

Se puede ver partidos de fútbol en el estadio

Se puede ver plantas y árboles en el jardín botánico

Se puede comer bien en el restaurante

Se puede hacer natación en la piscina

Se puede comprar ropa bonita en las tiendas del centro

Se puede montar en bici en el parque

Se puede ver películas en el cine cerca de mi casa

Se puede ver edificios históricos y castillos en el casco antiguo

7. Split sentences

Se puede ver películas

Se puede visitar edificios históricos

Se puede hacer natación en la piscina

Se puede ver partidos de fútbol

Se puede comer platos típicos

Se puede ir de compras

Se puede hacer deporte

Se puede montar en bici

8. Translate into English

a) go shopping   b) the old town   c) see matches   d) see movies   e) go to the stadium   f) the shops

g) the pedestrian street   h) ride the bike   i) go clubbing   j) go sightseeing   k) the main square

9. Faulty translation

a) The old town   b) A flamenco show   c) Old building   d) To go to the stadium   e) To go swimming   f) –

g) The pedestrian street   h) To go cycling   i) To see castles   j) To go clubbing   k) To go sightseeing   l) –

10. Spot and correct the grammar/spelling errors

a) Se puede ver espectáculos de flamenco   b) Se puede ver edificios históricos   c) Se puede **hacer** natación

d) Se puede visitar **un** castillo   e) Se puede montar **en** bici   f) Se puede **hacer** footing   g) Se puede visitar el **casco antiguo**

h) Se puede ver partidos de f**ú**tbol   i) Se puede **ver** una película en el cine   j) Se puede jugar al ten**i**s

11. Match

Visité un palacio histórico – I visited a historic palace   **Hice turismo** – I did sightseeing

Fui a la playa – I went to the beach   **Monté en bici** – I went cycling   **Vi una película** – I saw a film

El viernes pasado – Last Friday   **Anteayer** – The day before yesterday   **Hace tres días** – Three days ago

Ayer – Yesterday   **El fin de semana pasado** – Last weekend   **Fui de compras** – I went shopping

Hice deporte – I did sport   **Saqué muchas fotos** – I took many photos

12. Complete with the missing letters

a) Fui en b**ici**   b) H**i**ce deporte   c) **A**yer   d) Hice tur**ismo**   e) Fui a la p**laya**   f) Saqu**é** mucha**s** fotos

g) El fin de semana pas**ado**   h) Ante**ayer**   i) V**i** una pel**ícula**

13. Translate into English

a) The day before yesterday I visited a castle in the old town   b) Last Friday I went to the park with my family

c) Three days ago I went to the stadium to see a football match   d) Last Saturday I rode the bike in the park

e) Last Sunday I went to the swimming pool   f) Yesterday I played tennis in the tennis club near the school

g) Last week I went to the cinema with my girlfriend   h) Yesterday afternoon I saw an action film in TV

i) Last weekend I went shopping at the mall with my mother   j) Yesterday morning I didn't do anything

k) Yesterday I lifted weights with my uncle in the gym near my house

14. Spot and add in the missing words

a) Ayer visité **un** castillo   b) Anteayer fui **de** compras con mi hermana   c) El domingo pasado **no** hice nada

d) El viernes pasado fui **al** estadio   e) Hace tres días **hice** turismo en el centro de Madrid

f) Me encanta mi barrio porque **se** puede hacer muchas cosas   g) La semana pasada fui **al** centro comercial

h) Ayer por **la** tarde vi una película   i) Ayer monté **en** bici

15. Fill in the gaps

a) Vi **una** película

b) **Hice** deporte

c) **Jugué** al tenis

d) **Saqué** muchas fotos

e) Hice **deporte/turismo**

f) Fui de **compras**

g) Fui al **cine** para ver una película

h) Ayer **jugué** al fútbol con mis amigos

i) Anteayer fui al **estadio** a ver un partido de fútbol

j) Hace tres días monté en **bici** en el parque

k) Ayer **visité** un palacio histórico en el casco antiguo

l) Ayer por la mañana no **hice** nada

16. Find and correct the mistakes in the translation of Sergio's text

Hi. I'm Sergio. I live **on** the outskirts of the city, near the **countryside**. My neighbourhood is very **ugly**. There are many old and **dirty** buildings. There is not much to do for young people. **However**, there are some sports facilities such as **basketball** courts, a **tennis** club and a gym. Also, there is a **small** park. Therefore, one can **do sport**. Yesterday, I did a lot of **sport**. In the morning I rode **the bike** in the park and played **basketball**. In the afternoon I went **swimming** in the **sports centre** and after that I **lifted weights** with my best friend.

17. Find the Spanish equivalent of the following phrases in Mercedes' text

a) el casco antiguo   b) cerca del puerto   c) edificios históricos   d) muy bonitas   e) mercadillo   f) al aire libre

g) no hay mucho que hacer   h) se puede jugar   i) ayer fui de tiendas   j) compré   k) hice vela   l) fue muy divertido

m) fui al cine   n) vimos una película romántica

18. Read Mercedes' text and tick the words not mentioned

a) piscina   b) –   c)   d) –   e) cositas   f) supermercado   g) afueras   h) –   i) –   j) –   k) –   l) –

19. True, False or Not mentioned?

a) True   b) False   c) True   d) False   e) Not mentioned   f) True   g) False

20. Find the Spanish equivalent in the text

a) hay mucho que hacer   b) para los jóvenes   c) muchas tiendas bonitas   d) lugares históricos   e) cerca de la playa

f) se puede ir en bici   g) se puede ver partidos   h) se puede ir de compras   i) mucho más   j) ayer por la mañana

k) nadé   l) hice   m) fui de compras   n) monté en monopatín   o) fui a casa de mi amigo

21. Do the tasks below

a) bars ; restaurants ; shops ; sport facilities ; green spaces ; historic places ; main square ; stadium

b) one can ride the bike in the park ; one can see football matches in the stadium ; one can go swimming ;
one can go to the cinema ; and much more

c) swam ; lifted weights ; went shopping ; went skateboarding ; went to his friend's home to see a football match

22. Translate the words you can find in Roberto's text and cross out the rest

a) ~~casco antiguo~~   b) I rode   c) ~~natación~~   d) shopping   e) ~~enseguida~~   f) ~~por fin~~   g) then/afterwards   h) yesterday

i) morning   j) ~~tarde~~   k) near   l) ~~lejos~~   m) I went   n) see   o) match   p) ~~gente~~   q) the square   r) the young people

s) ~~los ancianos~~   t) weights   u) ~~con nosotros~~

23. Translate into Spanish

a) Casco antiguo   b) Ruido   c) Jóvenes   d) En la orilla/costa   e) Pasear   f) Instalaciones deportivas   g) Áreas verdes

h) Por lo tanto   i) Muchas cosas   j) Se puede comer bien   k) Se puede ir de paseo   l) Mucho más   m) Ayer por la mañana

n) Tomé el sol   o) Fui de compras   p) Jugar a los videojuegos

24. Correct any wrong statements about Fernando's text

a) His town is on the coast, near Barcelona   b) He lives by the sea shore   c) One can go to the park   d) The nightlife is great

e) There are many green spaces   f) He went shopping with his mother   g) He played videogames with Felipe

h) He watched a documentary about penguins

25. Complete the sentences in Spanish based on Fernando's text

a) Se llama **Fernando**   b) Su ciudad se llama **Tarragona**   c) El casco antiguo de su ciudad es muy **bonito**

d) Lo malo de Tarragona es que hay **mucho tráfico y ruido**   e) Su casa está en la **orilla del mar**

f) Las tiendas de su barrio son muy **bonitas**   g) En su barrio hay mucho que hacer para los **jóvenes**

h) Ayer jugó a **los videojuegos** en casa de su amigo Felipe

i) Este fin de semana Fernando va a ver un programa de televisión sobre unos **pingüinos** que viven en **Patagonia**

26. Complete with the missing letters

a) En mi b**arrio**   b) Se pueden/puede hacer muchas cosas   c) Se **puede comer** bien   d) Se **puede** ir de **compras**

e) Se **puede** ha**cer** d**eporte**   f) Se **puede** m**ontar** en b**ici**   g) Ayer f**ui** al **centro comercial**

h) Hace t**res** días v**i** u**na** pel**ícula**   i) Anteayer f**ui** al **estadio**

27. Sentence puzzle

a) Ayer fui al cine para ver una película   b) Anteayer monté en bici en el parque

c) En mi barrio se puede hacer deporte   d) Hace tres días fui al centro comercial

e) En mi barrio hay muchas tiendas bonitas   f) En mi barrio se puede hacer muchas cosas

g) Se puede jugar al frisbi en el parque

h) La semana pasada fui al *polideportivo   *Earlier edition says "centro polideportivo"

i) Ayer fui al estadio con mi hermano para ver un partido de fútbol

 **THE LANGUAGE GYM**

28. Complete with a suitable word

a) Ayer **fui** al cine para **ver** una **película** de acción

b) Anteayer **fui** de compras con mi **madre** en el **centro comercial** cerca de mi casa

c) En mi **barrio** se puede **hacer** muchísimas cosas

d) La semana pasada **monté** en bici en el **parque** cerca de mi casa

e) Vivo en el **casco** antiguo, la parte histórica de mi **ciudad**

f) En mi barrio **hay** una vida nocturna fenomenal. Se puede ir a **bares** y restaurantes al aire **libre**

g) El fin de **semana** pasado **fui** al centro **polideportivo** cerca de mi casa. **Hice** natación y **jugué** al bádminton con mis **amigos**

h) Se puede **visitar** muchos museos, galerías de **arte** y palacios **antiguos**

i) La semana pasada **fui** de paseo en el campo. Fue **maravilloso**

29. Translate into Spanish

a) El parque   b) Mi barrio   c) Hace tres días   d) Ayer   e) Anteayer   f) La semana pasada   g) Cerca de mi casa

h) Se puede comer   i) Un partido de fútbol   j) Al aire libre

30. Spot and correct the mistakes

a) *En mi barrio **se** puede hacer muchas cosas   b) *Se puede ver **muchos** monumentos   c) –   d) Mi barrio **está** en las afueras   e) Ayer yo fui al centro comercial cerca de mi casa f) Anteayer compré ropa en una tienda en el centro   g) Hace tres días yo hice pesas con mi mejor amigo   h) Se puede ir **al** estadio   i) Ayer por la mañana fui **de** paseo en la playa   j) –

*In early prints – A&B are both correct (-)

31. Complete

a) Nadé   b) Vi   c) Fui   d) Hice   e) Monté   f) Visité   g) Jugué

32. Translate into Spanish

a) En mi barrio se puede hacer muchas cosas   b) En mi pueblo/ciudad hay muchas tiendas y un mercadillo

c) Hay un parque grande cerca de mi casa   d) En el casco antiguo hay muchos edificios históricos y un palacio medieval

e) La vida nocturna es excelente. Hay muchos bares y restaurantes

f) Se puede hacer muchos deportes porque hay un polideportivo grande   g) Ayer hice vela con mi padre

h) Hace dos días monté en bici en el parque con mi mejor amigo

i) El fin de semana pasado fui de paseo por la playa con mi novia

j) La semana pasada hice turismo en Madrid. Saqué/tomé muchas fotos   k) Hace tres días fui al polideportivo y nadé

33. Write two paragraphs in the first person singular (I) about Yolanda and Luke

Accept any suitable answers for either text.

Question Skills Unit 2

1. Match questions and answers

¿Qué se puede hacer para estar en forma? – Se puede practicar deportes al aire libre

¿Qué instalaciones deportivas hay? – Hay un polideportivo muy bien equipado

¿Qué lugares de interés hay? – Hay un castillo árabe y una catedral

¿Cómo es tu barrio? – Es muy grande, moderno y tranquilo

¿Hay algún polideportivo en tu barrio? – No, no hay ningún sitio para practicar deporte

¿Qué hiciste el fin de semana pasado? – Hice footing y jugué al baloncesto

¿Hiciste algún deporte la semana pasada? – Sí, hice patinaje y monté en bici

¿Adónde fuiste el fin de semana pasado? – No fui a ninguna parte

2. Complete the questions with: *Adónde, Cómo, Cuánto, Cuándo, Dónde, Qué o Quién*

a) ¿**Cómo** se llama tu barrio?

b) ¿**Qué** es lo mejor de tu barrio?

c) ¿Desde **cuándo** vives allí?

d) ¿**Qué** lugares de interés hay?

e)¿**Dónde (accept adónde)** haces deporte normalmente?

f) ¿**Qué** hiciste ayer?

g) ¿**Cómo** pasaste el fin de semana pasado?

h) ¿**Adónde** fuiste el sábado?

i) ¿Con **quién** saliste?

j) ¿**Qué** fue lo mejor?

3. Sentence puzzle

a) ¿Qué se puede hacer en tu barrio?   b) ¿Qué hay en tu barrio para los jóvenes?   c) ¿Desde cuándo vives en este barrio?

d) ¿Qué lugares de interés hay en tu barrio?   e) ¿Qué hiciste el fin de semana pasado en tu barrio?

f) ¿Qué instalaciones deportivas hay en tu barrio?   g) ¿Con quién saliste el fin de semana pasado?

h) ¿Qué hiciste ayer en tu barrio?   i) ¿Qué deportes se pueden hacer en tu barrio?

4. Complete with a suitable word

a) ¿Qué se **puede** hacer en tu barrio?   b) ¿Qué **hiciste** el fin de semana pasado?   c) ¿Con quién **saliste** ayer?

d) ¿Cómo lo **pasaste**?   e) ¿Cómo es tu **barrio**?   f) ¿Desde cuándo **vives** allí?   g) ¿Dónde **está** tu barrio?

h) ¿**Hay** algún parque en tu barrio?

5. Write a question for each answer

a) ¿**Dónde está tu ciudad?** – Está en el norte del país

b) ¿**Cómo es tu ciudad?** – Es una ciudad industrial

c) ¿**Cómo se llama tu barrio?** – Mi barrio se llama Santa Lucía

d) ¿**Dónde está tu barrio?** – Está en las afueras de la ciudad

e) ¿**Qué hay en tu barrio?** – Hay polideportivos, piscinas y un estadio

f) ¿**Qué hiciste ayer?** – No hice mucho

g) ¿**Con quién saliste?** – Salí con mi novio

h) ¿**Qué fue lo mejor?** – Lo mejor fue el tiempo. Hizo sol

i) ¿**Qué fue lo peor?** – Lo peor fue que tuve que hacer los deberes

6. Guided translation

a) ¿Dónde **está** tu **b**arrio?   b) ¿Qué hay **para los jóvenes**?   c) ¿**Con** quién **saliste**?   d) ¿**Cómo** lo **pasaste**?

e) ¿**Hiciste** algún **de**porte?   f) ¿**Ad**ónde **fuiste**?

7. Translate into Spanish

a) ¿Qué atracciones turísticas hay?   b) ¿Qué se puede hacer para estar en forma?   c) ¿Qué hiciste el fin de semana pasado?

d) ¿Cómo es tu barrio?   e) ¿Con quién saliste?   f) ¿Qué hiciste la semana pasada?

Vocab Revision Workout 1

1. Match

La ciudad – The city   **El sur** – The South   **El país** – The country   **El barrio** – The neighbourhood
El rocódromo – The climbing wall   **El casco antiguo** – The old town   **Los edificios** – The buildings
Las afueras – The outskirts   **Las áreas verdes** – The green spaces   **La vida nocturna** – The nightlife
El estadio – The stadium

2. Complete with *hacer, jugar, ir, ver* or *visitar*

a) Se puede **hacer** natación   b) Se puede **ver** partidos de fútbol   c) Se puede **ir** de compras   d) Se puede **ver** conciertos
e) Se puede **visitar** palacios históricos   f) Se puede **jugar** al golf   g) Se puede **ver** películas   h) No se puede **ir** de marcha
i) No se puede **hacer** footing en el parque

3. Sentence puzzle

a) Hay una zona peatonal cerca de mi casa   b) En la calle peatonal hay muchas tiendas
c) En el casco antiguo hay muchas calles bonitas   d) Cerca de mi casa hay un rocódromo
e) Se puede hacer deporte en el polideportivo   f) Se pueden ver ruinas romanas en el casco antiguo
g) Cerca del puerto hay un castillo muy antiguo   h) Se puede hacer natación en la piscina municipal
i) En mi ciudad hay muchas cosas que hacer

4. Missing letters

a) Ayer   b) Hice   c) Se puede   d) Jugué   e) Vi   f) La calle   g) Mi barrio   h) Mi ciudad   i) Se puede ver
j) Pasear   k) Está sucio/a

5. Spot and correct the (many) spelling errors

a) Edimburgo está en Escocia   b) Cerca de mi casa hay una calle peatonal   c) En mi barrio hay un parque grande
d) Me gusta mi barrio porque es seguro   e) Mi barrio está limpio y bien cuidado   f) En mi barrio hay mucho tráfico
g) En mi barrio se puede hacer footing en el parque   h) Ayer jugué al tenis en un club cerca de mi casa
i) Anteayer hice natación en la piscina municipal   j) Hay muchos restaurantes...   k) ...donde se puede comer **bien**

6. Categories

Edificios: 7 ; 14 ; 16 ; 17   **Deportes:** 2 ; 3 ; 10 ; 13 ; 18   **Entretenimiento:** 4 ; 9 ; 11 ; 12   **Geografía:** 1 ; 5 ; 6 ; 8 ; 15

7. Match activity and place

Vi un partido de fútbol en el estadio   **Vi una película** en el cine   **Hice escalada** en el rocódromo
Hice natación en la piscina   **Fui de compras** en el centro comercial   **Hice turismo** en el casco antiguo
Hice pesas en el gimnasio   **Vi plantas exóticas** en el jardín botánico

8. Complete with a suitable word

a) Fui al centro **comercial**   b) Visité el **castillo**   c) Fui a ver un **partido**   d) Jugué al **tenis**   e) Hice **natación** en la piscina
f) Vi una **película** en el cine   g) Hice footing en el **parque**   h) Fui de **compras** en el centro comercial

9. Guided translation

a) **Vivo** en **Londres**   b) **Cerca** de mi **casa**   c) **En** mi **barrio** hay **muchos** jóvenes   d) Hay una **calle** peatonal bonita
e) Se **puede** hacer footing   f) Se **puede** ver películas   g) **Ayer** levanté/hice pesas

10. Translate into Spanish

a) Fui al centro comercial   b) Fui a ver un concierto   c) Vi una película en el cine   d) Nadé en la piscina
e) Visité un castillo antiguo   f) La semana pasada jugué al tenis
g) El fin de semana pasado fui de compras en la zona peatonal
h) Ayer fui a caminar con mi hermano en el bosque cerca de mi casa
i) Hace dos días hice turismo en el casco antiguo con mi novia

 THE LANGUAGE GYM

Unit 3: Describing my street

1. Match

A la derecha de – To the right of   **A la izquierda de** – To the left of   **Detrás de** – Behind   **Enfrente de** – Opposite to
Al lado de – Next to   **Cerca de** – Near   **Lejos de** – Far from   **En mi calle** – In my street   **Mi casa está** – My house is
En mi barrio – In my neighbourhood   **Mi edificio está** – My building is
A diez minutos en coche – Ten minutes away by car   **A cien metros de** – 100 metres away from
A diez minutos a pie – Ten minutes away on foot

2. Complete the translations

a) In my **street**   b) **Far** from   c) **100** metres away from   d) In my **neighbourhood**   e) My **house** is   f) Not **far** from
g) My **building**   h) Ten minutes away by **car**   i) **Next** to

3. Verdadero o falso

a) V   b) V   c) F   d) F   e) F   f) V   g) V   h) F

4. Faulty translation

a) In my street **there are** many shops   b) –   c) The tennis club is **opposite** the cinema
d) There are no clothes shops in my **street**   c) –   e) The park is behind the **train** station
f) There's a supermarket next to the **cinema**   g) The Chinese restaurant is 1 hour away **by car**

5. Break the flow

a) En mi calle no hay tiendas de ropa   b) Hay un restaurante a diez minutos a pie   c) La panadería está al lado de la carnicería
d) ¿Dónde está la biblioteca?   e) El restaurante chino está enfrente de la iglesia
f) Hay un campo de fútbol detrás de mi colegio   g) En mi calle hay muchas tiendas bonitas
h) Hay un restaurante muy bueno cerca de mi casa

6. Complete with the missing letters

a) Hay una igle**sia** cerca de mi ca**sa**   b) Al la**do** del supermercado hay un ci**ne**   c) Hay un parque det**rás** del restaurante
d) No hay tiendas de ro**pa** en mi calle   e) ¿Dón**de** está la biblio**te**ca?   f) Mi casa e**stá** enfrente del par**que**
g) La tien**da** está a la dere**cha** del cine   h) No ha**y** restaurantes por aq**uí**

7. Multiple choice

a) 2   b) 3   c) 1   d) 2   e) 1   f) 3   g) 2   h) 3   i) 2   j) 1   k) 2   l) 3

8. Location puzzle

Club de golf			Aparcamiento		
La casa de Marta	Supermercado	**Piscina municipal**	**Tienda de ropa**	Biblioteca	**Peluquería**
Calle Barbastro					
La casa de Paco	**Gran café Viñales**	Restaurante italiano	**Bar del Pingüino**	Cancha de baloncesto	**Cine Conti**
Campo de fútbol	Tienda de juguetes	Heladería	**Jardín**		Carnicería

9. Translate into English

a) Marcelo's house is opposite the train station   b) The local swimming pool is between the sports centre and the supermarket

c) The library is at the end of the street   d) To the right of the golf club there is a huge library

e) Behind the cinema there is a running track   f) Next to the cinema, to the left, there is a bus stop

g) To the left of my school there is a Chinese restaurant   h) Behind the police station there is a toy store

i) Next to Rafa's house there is a football field and a basketball court

j) Near my house there is a very big sports centre with an Olympic swimming pool

k) The stadium is very far from my house   l) I love my street because there are many shops

10. Find the Spanish equivalent

a) pero vivo   b) hay muchas cosas que hacer   c) instalaciones deportivas   d) *en mi calle hay   e) una pista de patinaje

f) hice pesas   g) fue muy agotador   h) hay muchas tiendas   i) a cinco minutos a pie   j) a cien metros de mi casa

k) al final de la calle   l) muy guay   m) compré un par de zapatillas   n) se puede comer bien

o) al lado de mi casa   p) a la derecha   q) comí en un restaurante chino

n.b. First run of books requires this answer: d) en mi habitación hay

11. Tick the items that you can find in Luisa's text and cross out the ones you can't

a) In my neighbourhood	f) Yesterday	k) Olympic swimming pool
b) A lot of sport	g) ~~Tomorrow~~	l) Sports shoes/trainers
c) ~~Music shop~~	h) Very funny	m) ~~A skirt~~
d) On the left	i) ~~To go jogging~~	n) Near
e) The food was very tasty	j) Clothes shop	o) My house

12. Answer the questions in English

a) Because there are many things to do   b) gym, skating rink, sports centre, Olympic swimming pool   c) lifting weights

d) five minutes away on foot   e) all sorts of things   f) at the end of the street   g) good   h) a Chinese restaurant

i) in the Chinese restaurant   j) very tasty   k) very cool   l) 100 metres away from her house

13. Find the Spanish equivalent

a) vivo en   b) una ciudad muy bonita   c) en las afueras   d) instalaciones deportivas   e) así que   f) un gimnasio muy viejo

g) pequeño y feo   h) no tiene ni piscina   i) ayer hice footing   j) el bosque   k) cerca de mi casa   l) no muy lejos de mi casa

m) a diez minutos en coche   n) se puede comprar de todo   o) aquí tengo muchos amigos   p) donde se puede comer muy bien

q) al lado de mi casa   r) a la izquierda   s) a la derecha

14. Answer providing as many details as possible

a) it's a very beautiful and historic city in the south of Spain   b) because there aren't many sports facilities

c) the gym is old and poorly equipped; the park is small, ugly and poorly kept; the sports centre is very bad, it doesn't have a swimming pool or a tennis court   d) yesterday he went jogging in the park and rode the bike in the forest near his home

e) not far from his home, a ten minute car ride away   f) all sorts of things   g) the videogames shops

h) he has a lot of friends here   i) an Italian restaurant   j) a Mexican restaurant   k) in the Mexican restaurant   l) tasty and spicy

15. Tick the items that you can find in Marcelo's text

b, c, d, g, h, j, l, m, n,

16. Translate into English

a) to the right of the school   b) near my house   c) opposite the cinema   d) in front of the supermarket

e) at the end of the street   f) not far from my house   g) next to the swimming pool   h) a 5 minute walk away

i) 100 meters from my house

17. Sentence puzzle

a) En mi barrio hay muchas tiendas   b) Hay un gimnasio al lado de mi casa   c) La piscina está al final de la calle

d) Mi colegio no está lejos de mi casa   e) El cine está entre el parque y la biblioteca

 **THE LANGUAGE GYM**

13

18. Find in the wordsearch

On the left – **A la izquierda**   It is near – **Está cerca**   On foot – **A pie**

By car – **En coche**   On the right there is – **A la derecha hay**   Near my house
– **Cerca de mi casa**   In my neighbourhood – **En mi barrio**

It isn't far – **No está lejos**   The shop – **La tienda**

At the end of the road – **Al final de la calle**

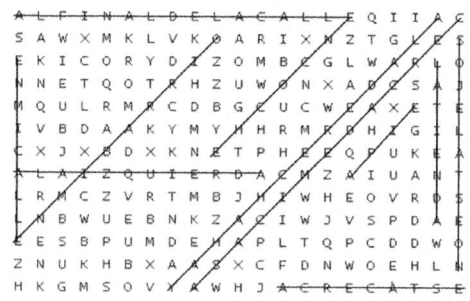

19. Tick the words below which are names of shops

a, d, e

20. Complete with the missing letters

a) Una pana**dería**   b) Una **car**nice**ría**   c) Un par**que**   d) Una bi**blio**te**ca**

e) Una tie**nda** de m**úsica**   f) Un e**dificio**   g) Una **tie**nda de **de**porte

21. Complete with the missing words

a) En mi calle hay muchas **tiendas**   b) La panadería está a cinco minutos a **pie**   c) La biblioteca está al **lado** de mi colegio

d) La **carnicería** está allí, a la **derecha**   e) Mi coche está **delante** del supermercado   f) El estadio está muy **lejos** de mi casa

g) La piscina está al **final** de la calle   h) En mi **calle** no hay muchas **tiendas**   i) **Detrás** de mi edificio hay un parque

22. Translate into Spanish

a) **Al lado** de mi **casa**   b) **Enfrente** de mi **edificio**   c) **Lejos** de a**quí**   d) A la **derecha**   e) A la **izquierda**

f) **Cerca** de mi **casa**   g) **Detrás** de la **carnicería**   h) **Al lado** de la **panadería**

23. Write a paragraph

Accept any suitable answers.

THE LANGUAGE GYM

Question Skills Unit 3

1. Match questions and answers

¿Te gusta tu barrio? – No, odio vivir aquí

¿Qué hiciste en tu barrio recientemente? – Fui al parque con mis amigos

¿Por qué no te gusta tu barrio? – Porque es muy ruidoso y no es seguro

¿Qué tiendas hay? – Hay de todo: tiendas de ropa, de música, etc.

¿Dónde está tu barrio? – Está cerca del centro de la ciudad

¿Qué hay al lado de tu casa? – Hay un restaurante chino muy bueno

¿Qué hay para los jóvenes? – Hay un parque temático y un club de jóvenes

¿Tu colegio está lejos de tu casa? – No, está muy cerca, a diez minutos a pie

¿En qué calle está tu casa? – En la Avenida Salvador Dalí

¿Hay instalaciones deportivas en tu barrio? – Sí. Por ejemplo, hay un polideportivo

2. Complete with the missing words

a) ¿Cómo se ll**ama** tu calle?   b) ¿Dónde e**stá** tu calle?   c) ¿Te g**usta** tu barrio?   d) ¿Por qu**é** no te gusta?

e) ¿Qué hay para los j**óvenes**?   f) ¿Qué **tiendas** hay en tu barrio?   g) ¿**Hay** instalaciones deportivas?

h) ¿Qué hay e**nfrente** de tu casa?   i) ¿Hay algún parque **cerca** de tu casa?   j) ¿Tu colegio está l**ejos** de tu casa?

3. Split questions

¿Cómo se llama tu barrio?

¿Dónde está tu piso?

¿Hay instalaciones deportivas?

¿Por qué no te gusta tu barrio?

¿Desde cuándo vives allí?

¿Qué hay para los jóvenes?

¿Qué lugares de interés hay en tu barrio?

¿Con quién saliste?

¿Adónde fuiste ayer?

¿Qué es lo mejor de donde vives?

4. Translate into English

a) What is your neighbourhood called?   b) In which part of the city is it located?

c) Tell me about your neighbourhood. Do you like it?   d) Are there sports facilities?   e) What is there for young people?

f) What is the worst thing about your neighbourhood? And the best thing?   g) What is there opposite your house?

h) What is there next to your house?   i) What did you do last weekend?   j) Where did you go? With whom? How was it?

k) Since when/how long have you lived there?

5. Guided translation

a) ¿C**ómo** se llama tu **barrio**?   b) ¿Dónde e**stá** si**tuado**?   c) ¿Qué **hay** e**n** tu **barrio**?   d) ¿Qué e**s** lo me**jor**?

e) ¿**Desde** c**uándo**?   f) ...el f**in** de s**emana** pasado?   g) ¿A**dónde** f**uiste**? ¿C**on** quién?   h) ¿Cómo lo p**asaste**?

THE LANGUAGE GYM

Unit 4: Describing my home and furniture

1. Translate into English

a) in the countryside   b) in the outskirts   c) in the kitchen   d) in the living room   e) in the playroom   f) in the attic
g) in the garden   h) in the garage   i) in my bedroom   j) in my parents' bedroom   k) in my brother's bedroom
l) in the basement

2. Match

Una despensa – A pantry   **Una cama** – A bed   **Una estantería** – A bookshelf   **Una silla** – A chair
Un sillón – An armchair   **Un escritorio** – A desk   **Una alfombra** – A carpet   **Una televisión** – A television
Una nevera – A fridge   **Un horno** – An oven   **Unas cortinas** – Curtains

3. Write, in Spanish, in which rooms the following objects are most likely to be found

a) el salón, el comedor   b) la habitación, el dormitorio   c) el salón, la habitación, el dormitorio   d) el salón
e) el cuarto de baño   f) el cuarto de baño   g) la cocina   h) la habitación, el dormitorio   i) la habitación, el dormitorio
j) la sala de juegos   k) el dormitorio   l) el salón, el comedor   m) el garaje   n) el jardín
o) el salón, el comedor, el dormitorio   p) el cuarto de baño

4. Complete with the missing letters

a) La du**cha**   b) La me**sa**   c) La ca**ma**   d) El escri**torio**   e) El **ár**bol   f) La si**lla**   g) Los jugu**etes**

5. Write Probable (likely) or Improbable (unlikely)

a) Improbable   b) Probable   c) Improbable   d) Improbable   e) Probable

6. Multiple choice

a) 1   b) 3   c) 2   d) 1   e) 2   f) 3   g) 1   h) 2   i) 1   j) 2   k) 3

7. Faulty translation

a) In the kitchen there is a table and four chairs   b) In my bedroom there are red curtains   c) –
d) In our garden there aren't any trees   e) –   f) Beside my bed there is a small table   g) The mirror is near the door
h) –   i) En la cocina hay un armario grande. In the kitchen there is a big wardrobe

8. Spot the hidden phrases, fill in the gaps and translate into English

a) Un d**ormitorio** p**equeño** – A small bedroom   b) Una **cama grande** – A big bed   c) Un j**ardín verd**e – A green garden
d) Una **cocina limpi**a – A clean kitchen   e) Un **dormi**torio m**oderno** – A modern bedroom
f) Un c**omedor** muy b**onito** – A very beautiful living room   g) Un s**alón** b**ien** am**ueblado** – A well-furnished living room

9. Write Verdadero (true) or Falso (false)

a) Verdadero   b) Falso   c) Falso   d) Verdadero   e) Falso   f) Verdadero   g) Verdadero   h) Falso   i) Falso
j) Verdadero   k) Verdadero

10. Answer the questions in English

a) On the outskirts   b) Climbing wall, skating rink, slide   c) Often   d) Play frisbee, go jogging, ride the bike
e) Gym, swimming pool   f) Seventh floor   g) Kitchen, living room, two bathrooms, playroom, three bedrooms
h) Because it's very cosy and well decorated   i) Bedside table and armchair   j) Wardrobe   k) Desk   l) The TV
m) Listens to music, reads books and magazines, does his homework

11. Find the Spanish equivalent

a) cerca de mi casa   b) un rocódromo   c) montar en bici   d) a cien metros a pie   e) en la séptima planta
f) una sala de juegos   g) es muy acogedor   h) el dormitorio de mi hermana mayor   i) al otro lado   j) en la esquina
k) detrás de la televisión   l) a la derecha de la ventana

12. Spot the FIVE words on the list below which are not contained in Pedro's text

a) Moto   j) Desván   k) Lejos   m) Luminoso   o) Paseo

13. Complete the sentences based on Paco's text

a) He lives with his family in a historic building in the centre of the city   b) In the parks there is a lot of space to play

c) In his neighbourhood there are many monuments, theatres, cinemas, restaurants, outdoors bars, many beautiful shops and a big aquarium   d) His building is very old

e) In his flat there are a kitchen, a living room, a dining room, two bathrooms, a playroom and two bedrooms

f) His favourite room is his bedroom because it's very cosy   g) The bed is big and comfy

h) To the right of the bed there is a bedside table and a mirror   i) There is a big wardrobe in the corner

j) The TV is small but new   k) Behind the TV there is a very large window

14. Faulty translation

My favourite room is my bedroom because it is very **cosy** and is very well furnished and decorated. There is a very big and **comfy** bed. To the left of the bed there is a very spacious **desk**. To the right there is a **bedside/night** table and a **mirror**. On the other side of the room, in the corner, there is a huge **wardrobe**. Next to the wardrobe, **opposite** the bed, there is my computer and a TV. The TV is very small, but is **new**. **Behind** the TV there is a very large window. To the right of the window there is an armchair. I spend a lot of time in my bedroom listening to music, **playing in my computer**, playing the guitar, **reading** and doing my homework.

15. List as many words from Paco's text as possible, under the following headings

Adjectives: histórico, bonito, antiguo, acogedor, grande, cómoda, espacioso, enorme, pequeña, nueva, grande

Furniture: cama, escritorio, mesita de noche, espejo, armario, sillón

Verbs: me llamo, vivo, me encanta, hay, ver, hacer, jugar, voy, es, paso, escuchando, jugando, tocando, leyendo, haciendo

Locative adverbs/prepositions: cerca de, a la izquierda de, a la derecha de, al otro lado de, al lado de, enfrente de, detrás de

16. Arrange the words in each sentence in the correct order

a) En mi dormitorio no hay ni una televisión ni un ordenador

b) En la cocina hay una mesa, dos sillas, una nevera, un horno y una alacena

c) En el salón hay dos sillones, una alfombra, un sofá y una televisión

d) No hay sillas en mi dormitorio pero hay un sillón muy cómodo

e) El espejo está al lado de la puerta y la ventana está detrás del escritorio

17. Translate into Spanish

a) Una **silla bonita**   b) Una **cocina luminosa**   c) Una **alfombra roja**   d) Unas **cortinas azules**   e) Un **piso espacioso**

f) Un **armario viejo**   g) Una **cama cómoda**   h) Un **edificio**   i) Una **televisión nueva**

18. Complete with a suitable word (accept any other correct suggestions)

a) En mi barrio hay muchas **tiendas buenas, etc.**   b) Mi habitación favorita es la **cocina** porque es **luminosa, espaciosa, etc.**

c) Al lado del armario hay una **silla, televisión, etc.**   d) El espejo **está** al lado de la **puerta, ventana, etc.**

e) En mi casa **hay** siete habitaciones

19. Insert *de la* o *del* as appropriate

a) de la   b) del   c) de la   d) del   e) del   f) del   g) de la   h) del

20. Spot and add the missing words

a) La cocina **está** al lado del comedor   b) En mi casa **hay** siete habitaciones   c) En el salón hay **una** alfombra roja

d) Vivo **en** un edificio antiguo   e) El espejo está **al** lado de la puerta   f) Me encanta **la** cocina

g) La televisión está enfrente **de** mi cama   h) El dormitorio de **mis** padres es muy grande

21. Translate into Spanish

a) En mi **piso hay seis habitaciones**   b) Mi **habitación favorita** es...   c) **También** me encanta mi **dormitorio**

d) Mi **dormitorio** es muy **acogedor**   e) **También** hay un **escritorio grande**   f) Hay una **cama grande** y **cómoda**

g) Vivo en un **edificio moderno**   h) No me **gusta** mi **salón**

 **THE LANGUAGE GYM**

17

22. Spot and correct the errors

a) En mi dormitorio **hay** un escritorio muy grande   b) En mi casa hay seis habitaci**ones**

c) En mi barrio hay muchas **tiendas buenas**   d) Mi **habitación** favorita **es** el salón

e) Mi habitación es muy grande y acogedor**a**   f) Vivo **en** un edificio antiguo   g) El salón **está** muy bien amueblado

h) Al lado de **la/mi** cama hay una mesita **de** noche   i) Me encanta mi casa porque **es** muy bonita

23. Complete each sentence with an appropriate verb

a) llama b) es   c) está d) hay   e) puede; hacer; comprar   f) encanta   g) está   h) paso   i) hago   j) juego   k) monto

l) gusta

24. Translate into Spanish

Vivo en un barrio bonito en las afueras de Sevilla, una ciudad en el sur de España. Me gusta mucho mi barrio porque hay muchas cosas que hacer para la gente de mi edad. Hay muchas tiendas buenas, dos parques bonitos, tres centros comerciales grandes y muchas instalaciones deportivas. También hay muchos bares y restaurantes.

Vivo en un piso grande en un edificio moderno. En mi piso hay siete habitaciones. Mi habitación favorita es mi dormitorio porque es espacioso y está bien amueblado. También, la cama es grande y cómoda y hay un escritorio grande con un ordenador nuevo.

25. Write two 80-100 word paragraphs in the first person

Vivo en Bilbao. Mi barrio está en el centro de la ciudad. Me gusta mi barrio porque hay muchas tiendas buenas e instalaciones deportivas excelentes. Hay muchos bares y restaurantes, y hay un parque bonito cerca de mi casa. Vivo en un piso con siete habitaciones y mi habitación favorita es mi dormitorio, porque es espacioso, luminoso y está bien amueblado. Odio el salón porque está mal amueblado, es pequeño y el sofá es viejo y feo.

Mi casa es grande y moderna. Me encanta mi salón porque está bien amueblado y es luminoso. En el salón hay un sofá grande. Al lado del sofá hay una mesa pequeña/mesita y enfrente del sofá hay una televisión. También me encanta mi dormitorio porque es acogedor. En mi dormitorio hay una cama grande y cómoda. Al lado de la cama hay una mesita de noche y al lado de la mesita de noche hay un armario enorme. Enfrente del armario hay un escritorio grande con un ordenador.

26. Write a paragraph in Spanish in the first person

Vivo en Buenos Aires, la capital de Argentina. Vivo en las afueras, en un barrio residencial. Me gusta mi barrio porque se puede hacer mucho deporte. Hay muchas instalaciones deportivas, como gimnasios, un polideportivo, dos campos de fútbol, algunos clubs de tenis y golf, algunas piscinas y un estadio. También hay un centro comercial enorme, un parque bonito y un río. El fin de semana pasado hice mucho deporte. Hice ciclismo en el parque, hice pesas en el gimnasio, jugué al fútbol con mis amigos del colegio y fui a mi centro comercial favorito con mi novio/novia. Lo pasé muy bien. En mi calle hay muchas tiendas y restaurantes buenos. Por ejemplo, hay un restaurante italiano bueno al lado de mi casa. En mi piso hay siete habitaciones: una cocina, dos cuartos de baño, tres dormitorios y un salón. Mi habitación favorita es el salón, porque es grande, está bien amueblado y es luminoso. También hay un sofá muy cómodo y una televisión nueva. El sofá está enfrente de la televisión. A la izquierda del sofá hay un sillón y a su derecha hay una planta grande. Delante del sofá hay una pequeña mesa/mesita negra. Entre el sofá y la televisión hay una alfombra vieja.

Question Skills Unit 4

1. Faulty translation
a) Do you live in a building?   b) Describe your bedroom   c) –   d) Do you share your room with someone?
e) What do you like about your bedroom?   f) How many bedrooms are there?   g) How many rooms are there in your house?
h) Why don't you like the living room?   i) –   j) Is there any playroom in your house?

2. Complete with the missing words
a) ¿**Qué** hay en tu dormitorio?   b) ¿**Cuántas** habitaciones hay en tu piso?   c) ¿**Cuál** es tu habitación favorita?
d) ¿En **qué** habitación haces tus deberes?   e) ¿**Por qué** no te gusta tu habitación?   f) ¿Desde **cuándo** vives allí?
g) ¿Con **quién** vives?   h) ¿**Hay** una sala de juegos en tu casa?   i) ¿**Tienes** pósteres en tu habitación?
j) ¿Qué es lo que más **te gusta** de tu casa?

3. Match questions and answers
¿**Vives en una casa o en un piso?** – Vivo en una casa

¿**Cuántas habitaciones hay en tu casa?** – Hay siete habitaciones en total

¿**Desde cuándo vives allí?** – Desde hace cinco años

¿**Cuál es tu habitación favorita? ¿Por qué?** – Prefiero el salón, porque es muy espacioso

¿**En qué habitación pasas más tiempo?** – Paso horas y horas en mi dormitorio

¿**Dónde haces tus deberes?** – El trabajo escolar lo hago en el salón

Describe tu dormitorio – Es pequeño pero muy acogedor

¿**Compartes tu dormitorio con alguien?** – Sí, lo comparto con mi hermano mayor

¿**Qué te gusta más de tu dormitorio?** – ¡Lo mejor de mi dormitorio es mi cama grande!

¿**Cómo es la cocina?** – Es bonita y hay una nevera grande

4. Guided translation
a) **Describe tu dormitorio**   b) ¿**Vives en una casa o en un piso?**   c) ¿**Dónde haces tus deberes?**   d) ¿**Con quién vives?**
e) ¿**Compartes tu dormitorio?**   f) ¿**Te gusta tu casa?**   g) ¿**Desde cuándo vives aquí?**   h) ¿**Cuál es tu habitación favorita?**

Vocab Revision Workout 2

1. Match

Al final de – At the end of   **Al lado de** – Next to   **Detrás de** – Behind   **Lejos de** – Far from

A diez minutos a pie – A ten minute walk   **Enfrente de** – Opposite   **Cerca de** – Near   **A la derecha de** – To the right of

A la izquierda de – To the left of   **En la esquina de** – On the corner of   **Delante de** – In front of

A diez minutos en coche – A ten minute car ride

2. Missing letters

a) Hay una biblio**teca**   b) Hay un cam**po** de fútbol   c) Hay una panad**ería**   d) Hay un supermerc**ado**

e) Hay una tien**da** de ropa   f) No hay ninguna igle**sia**   g) No hay ninguna pisc**ina**   h) Vivo en un **edificio**   i) Voy al tea**tro**

j) Mi colegio está a la izqu**ierda**   k) Mi casa está a la dere**cha**   l) La tienda está al final de la ca**lle**

3. Break the flow

a) Cerca de mi casa hay un parque pequeño   b) En mi casa hay cinco habitaciones   c) En mi calle hay muchas tiendas buenas

d) Vivo en el norte de España, cerca de Barcelona   e) Me gusta mi barrio porque hay muchas cosas que hacer

f) Vivo en una ciudad turística en el sur del país   g) No hay ningún restaurante cerca de donde vivo

h) Mi casa está entre la carnicería y el supermercado

4. Write an A next to the adjectives and an N next to the nouns

a) A   b) A   c) N   d) A   e) A   f) N   g) N   h) N   i) A   j) A   k) N   l) N   m) N   n) A   o) N   p) N   q) N   r) A

5. Spot the incorrect translations and fix them. Note: not all the translations are wrong

a) –   b) I live in an industrial neighbourhood   c) In my bedroom there are blue curtains   d) My house is next to the butcher's

e) In my kitchen there is a very big oven   f) –   g) My flat is in a modern building

h) Near my house there is a very beautiful park   i) At the end of the street there is a supermarket

j) In my building there are seven floors

6. Complete

a) **Cerca** de mi casa   b) En mi **barrio**   c) Hay mucho **ruido**   d) Ayer h**ice** footing   e) Al final de la **calle**

f) Vivo en un **piso**   g) En mi **pueblo**   h) Mi casa es b**onita**   i) Un **armario** grande

7. Complete with *fui, jugué, hice* o *vi*

a) **Vi** una película en el cine   b) **Fui** al parque con mi perro   c) **Jugué** al tenis en el polideportivo

d) **Hice** escalada en el parque   e) No **hice** nada ayer   f) **Jugué** al baloncesto en el colegio   g) **Fui** al estadio a ver un partido

h) **Vi** dibujos animados   i) **Hice** pesas en el gimnasio   j) **Hice** turismo en el casco antiguo

8. Slalom writing

a) Ayer fui a la piscina solo   b) En mi pueblo hay mucho que hacer   c) En mi dormitorio hay un escritorio

d) Hace dos días no hice nada   e) La biblioteca está enfrente de la tienda   f) Mi salón es bastante espacioso

g) Está a cinco minutos a pie

9. Translate into Spanish

a) Vivo en el noreste de España, en la costa   b) Vivo en un barrio en las afueras   c) Vivo con mis padres y mis dos hermanos

d) Mi barrio es aburrido y peligroso   e) No hay nada que hacer para los jóvenes

f) Solo hay un polideportivo y unas pocas tiendas   g) El fin de semana pasado jugué al tenis y al baloncesto

h) También fui al centro. Vi una película

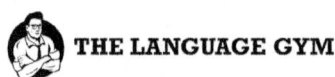 **THE LANGUAGE GYM**

Unit 5: Saying what I did & am going to do at the weekend

1. Match

Vamos a ir de compras – We are going to go shopping

Vamos a jugar al baloncesto – We are going to play basketball

Vamos a ver una película – We are going to watch a film

Vamos a leer un libro – We are going to read a book

Vamos a hacer deporte – We are going to do sport

Vamos a hacer natación –We are going to go swimming

Vamos a ir al estadio – We are going to go to the stadium

Vamos a hacer los deberes – We are going to do homework

Vamos a jugar a los videojuegos – We are going to play videogames

Vamos a ver un concierto – We are going to see a concert

Vamos a montar en bici – We are going to ride the bike

2. Complete with *ir, hacer, jugar, montar* or *ver*

a) Voy a **ir** de compras   b) Voy a **ver** un concierto   c) Vamos a **jugar** al tenis   d) Vamos a **ir** al centro comercial

e) Voy a **ir** al campo   f) Voy a **hacer** deporte   g) Voy a **ver** una película en el cine   h) Voy a **ir** al estadio

i) Voy a **montar** a caballo en el campo

3. Complete with the missing letters

a) Voy a ver una película   b) Voy a ir al estadio   c) Vamos a hacer deporte   d) Vamos a jugar al baloncesto

e) Voy a ir al parque   f) Será divertido   g) Vamos a montar a caballo   h) Vamos a ir al centro comercial

i) Vamos a hacer natación   j) Voy a montar en bici

4. Faulty translation: correct the mistakes in the translations below (not all are wrong!)

a) Next **Saturday** I am going to watch a film   b) Next weekend **we are** going to **ride a bike**   c) -

d) Sunday **afternoon** I am going to shopping   e) Next Saturday my aunt is going to go to the **pool**

f) On Friday **I am** going to do **my** homework   g) I am going to go out with my friend in the **morning**

5. Sentence puzzle

a) El sábado próximo vamos a ir al estadio   b) El fin de semana próximo voy a ir al centro comercial

c) El fin de semana próximo vamos a ir de compras   d) El domingo por la mañana voy a ir a la iglesia

e) Mis padres van a ver una película en el cine   f) Mi hermana va a ir a la piscina con sus amigas

g) El viernes próximo mi hermano va a ir de marcha

6. Multiple choice

a) 2   b) 2   c) 3   d) 1   e) 2   f) 1   g) 3   h) 1   i) 3

7. Find in the wordsearch

a) Aburrido   b) Apasionante

c) Será   d) No hacer nada

e) Hacer deporte   f) Dar un paseo

g) Jugar   h) Montar en bici

i) Montar a caballo   j) Ver una película

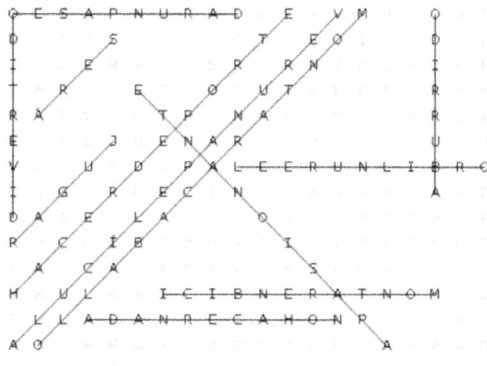

THE LANGUAGE GYM

8. Translate into English

a) Next Saturday my girlfriend and I are going to see a film

b) Next weekend my brother and I are going to play badminton

c) Next Friday my parents are going to see a flamenco show

d) Next Sunday afternoon/evening I'm going to go shopping with my mother

e) Next weekend my sister is going to go to the swimming pool with her boyfriend

f) Next weekend I'm going to do my math homework

g) Next Saturday morning I'm going to go to the park with my younger brother

h) Afterwards, my brother and I are going to eat in the Italian restaurant near my house

9. Match

Fui de compras – I went shopping   **Leí un libro** – I read a book   **Vi una película** – I watched a film

Monté a caballo – I rode a horse   **No hice nada** – I didn't do anything   **Fui a la biblioteca** – I went to the library

Hicimos deporte – We did sport   **Jugué al baloncesto** – I played basketball   **Jugamos al tenis** – We played tennis

Hicimos footing – We went jogging   **No hicimos nada** – We didn't do anything

10. Complete with the missing letters

a) Fui de compras   b) Fuimos al campo   c) Hicimos deporte   d) Vi una película   e) Fui al estadio   f) Leí un libro

g) Jugamos al baloncesto   h) Vimos monumentos   i) No hice nada

11. Choose the correct verb and cross out the wrong ones

a) ~~Hice~~ / ~~Vi~~ / **Jugué** al baloncesto   b) **No hice** / ~~vi~~ / ~~jugué~~ nada   c) **Monté** / ~~Vi~~ / ~~Hice~~ en bici   d) ~~Fui~~ / ~~Vi~~ / **Escuché** música

e) ~~Vi~~ / ~~Jugué~~/ **Fui** de compras   f) **No vi** / ~~jugué~~ / ~~hice~~ nada   g) **Hicimos** / ~~Vimos~~ / ~~Fuimos~~ pesas   h) ~~Vi~~ / ~~Hice~~ / **Leí** un libro

12. Anagrams

a) Fui de compras   b) Vi una película   c) No hice nada   d) Jugué al baloncesto   e) Fuimos al estadio   f) Hicimos deporte

g) No hice mis deberes   h) Jugamos al tenis

13. Slalom writing

a) El sábado pasado fui de compras con mi novia   b) El viernes pasado hice mis deberes después del colegio

c) El domingo pasado no hice nada. Solo vi una película   d) Hace tres días fui al gimnasio con mi hermano mayor

e) Anteayer jugué al baloncesto con mis amigos   f) El sábado próximo voy a ir al estadio con mi primo

g) El viernes próximo voy a hacer turismo en el casco antiguo

14. Translate into English

a) I went to the swimming pool   b) I am going to go shopping   c) We went to the bowling alley

d) My friend and I did sport   e) We are going to ride the bike   f) I went swimming   g) I am going to go to the stadium

h) We played basketball   i) We went sightseeing   j) We ate tapas   k) I read a novel   l) We saw cartoons

m) We went to the stadium   n) I went for a walk in the park

15. Complete the hidden sentences

a) **Monté en bici**   b) **Fui de compras**   c) **Jugué al baloncesto**   d) **Fuimes a la bolera**   e) **Fui al estadio**   f) **No hice nada**

g) **Hice mis deberes**   h) **Jugamos al tenis**   i) **Fui a la piscina**   j) **Monté a caballo**   k) **Leí una novela**

16. Complete the table

a) pasado, bici, parque   b) viernes, vi, tele   c) el, compras, centro   d) ayer, hice, piscina   e) Hace, película, cine

f) pasada, jugué, colegio   g) semana, fui, amigo

17. Complete the table

Fuimos de compras ; Hice mis deberes ; Hago mis deberes ; Voy a montar en monopatín ; Fui al estadio ; Voy a ir al estadio ;

Monté a caballo ; Voy a montar a caballo ; Voy a ir a una fiesta ; Monté en bici ; Vi una película ; Voy a ver una película ;

Veo dibujos animados ; Voy a ver dibujos animados

18. Find in the text the Spanish equivalent

a) no hice nada especial   b) volví a mi casa   c) comí un bocadillo   d) hice mis deberes   e) fui al gimnasio   f) fue agotador
g) vi una película   h) no fue nada apasionante   i) fui de compras   j) por la tarde   k) monté en bici   l) con mi novia
m) lo pasé muy bien con ella   n) es muy inteligente y graciosa   o) fui a la iglesia   p) después me relajé   q) nada especial

19. Answer the questions in the first person

a) El viernes volví a casa a eso de las cuatro   b) Comí un bocadillo   c) Escuché música   d) Con mi hermano mayor
e) Agotador pero divertido   f) Vi una película de acción   g) Fui de compras   h) Con mi madre
i) Compré una camiseta y unos vaqueros   j) A eso de las siete   k) Es muy inteligente y graciosa   l) Fui a la iglesia

20. Spot and correct the mistakes in these sentences from Sergio's text

a) No hice nada **e**special   b) El viernes, despu**é**s **del** colegio, volv**í** a casa a eso de las cuatro   c) Com**í** un bocadillo **de** queso
d) Hice mis deberes y fui al gimnasio   e) **Vi** una pel**í**cula   f) El s**á**bado por la ma**ñ**ana   g) Fui de compras
h) Compr**é** una camiseta   i) El domingo **no** hice nada   j) Me levant**é** tarde   k) Me relaj**é** escucha**ndo** música
l) Fu**e** un fin de semana muy relajante

21. Tick the phrases below that are contained in Amparo's text

a ; e ; f ; g ; h ; j ; l

22. *Amparo, Ana* or *Neither* of them?

a) Amparo   b) Amparo   c) Ana   d) Neither   e) Ana   f) Ana   g) Amparo   h) Ana   i) Amparo   j) Ana

23. Find the Spanish equivalent

a) por la mañana   b) hice mis deberes   c) al lado de mi casa   d) no hice nada especial   e) temprano
f) estoy intentando estar en forma   g) con mi mejor amiga   h) miramos escaparates   i) comimos muy bien
j) fui a mi tienda (de ropa) favorita   k) me relajé

24. Translate the words

a) I went out   b) cool   c) we ate   d) early   e) we looked at   f) I'm trying to   g) listening to music

25. Find someone who...

a) Julián   b) Silvia   c) Paco   d) Julián   e) Paco   f) Paco   g) Marcela   h) Silvia   i) Susana   j) Julián   k) Marcela

26. Find the Spanish equivalent

a) el domingo pasado   b) fui a la biblioteca   c) cuando terminé mis deberes   d) fue bastante aburrido
e) ayudé a mi madre con las tareas domésticas   f) cenamos allí   g) hice mucho deporte   h) con mis mejores amigos
i) el parque de mi barrio   j) hice pesas   k) todavía me duelen los brazos

27. Tick or cross?

a) **Lo pasé muy bien**	f) **Lo pasamos bomba**	k) **Hice pesas**
b) ~~Hice vela~~	g) ~~Fue interesante~~	l) **Por la mañana**
c) ~~Saqué muchas fotos~~	h) **Tomamos algo**	m) **Hicimos turismo**
d) ~~Monté en bici~~	i) **El casco antiguo**	n) **No hice nada de nada**
e) **Cenamos allí**	j) ~~Fui a la piscina~~	o) ~~Me metí en internet~~

28. Sentence puzzle

a) Me levanté temprano   b) Saqué muchas fotos   c) No hice nada especial   d) Fui al cine solo
e) Me relajé escuchando música   f) Hicimos turismo en el centro   g) Hicimos ciclismo en el campo
h) Hicimos senderismo en las colinas   i) El sábado pasado fuimos de compras   j) Por la tarde salí con mi novia

29. Complete the translation

a) Lo pasé **bomba**   b) Fui al **casco** antiguo   c) El **sábado** pasado   d) Monté en **bici**   e) Hicimos **turismo**
f) Fui al **estadio** con mi **padre**   g) Me **relajé** escuchando **música**   h) No **hice** nada **especial**   i) Me levanté **tarde**
j) **Por** la mañana fui al parque

30. Rewrite the sentences on the left in the preterite and the right in the near future

Fui al estadio	Voy a ir al estadio
Hice mis deberes	Voy a hacer mis deberes
Monté a caballo	Voy a montar a caballo
Jugué al baloncesto	Voy a jugar al baloncesto
Lo pasé bomba	Voy a pasarlo bomba
Comí un bocadillo	Voy a comer un bocadillo
Escuché música	Voy a escuchar música

31. Split sentences

Comí carne y ensalada ; **Me relajé** leyendo ; **No hice** nada ; **Compré** un vestido rosa ; **Vi** un partido de fútbol en la tele ; **Fui** al centro comercial ; **Hice natación** en la piscina municipal ; **Me levanté** temprano ; **Monté** en bici ; **Jugué** al baloncesto

32. Translate into Spanish

a) Lo pasé bomba   b) Fui al cine   c) Hicimos turismo   d) Voy a jugar al baloncesto   e) No hice nada

f) Fuimos de compras   g) Vamos a ir a una fiesta   h) Monté en mi bici

33. Complete with the missing verbs

a) **Fui** al parque con mi perro   b) **Compré** una camiseta   c) Ayer **vi** una serie en la tele   d) **Monté** en bici en el parque

e) **Jugué** a las cartas con mi abuelo   f) Me **relajé** escuchando música   g) El sábado me **levanté** temprano

h) **Fui** a la fiesta de mi primo   i) No **hice** nada el domingo pasado   j) **Jugué** al tenis   k) **Saqué** muchas fotos

l) **Fui** al estadio con mi padre   m) **Leí** una revista en el salón

34. Write a paragraph

Se puede ver muchas cosas en mi barrio. Por ejemplo, hay muchas tiendas (bonitas/buenas), un castillo medieval y un museo grande. Además, se puede comer bien, ir de compras, ver conciertos e ir al cine. También hay muchas instalaciones deportivas, como un polideportivo grande, gimnasios, una piscina y un rocódromo. El fin de semana pasado fui de compras, vi un partido de fútbol y fui a una fiesta en la casa de un amigo/amiga. El fin de semana próximo voy a ir a un concierto, voy a jugar al baloncesto con mis amigos y voy a hacer turismo en el casco antiguo.

35. Write a 200 word description of your neighbourhood

Accept any suitable answers.

Question Skills Unit 5

1. Sentence puzzle

a) ¿Con quién vas a ir?

b) ¿Qué vas a hacer el fin de semana próximo?

c) ¿Qué tiempo hizo?

d) ¿Qué deporte hiciste?

e) ¿Qué hiciste el fin de semana pasado?

f) ¿A qué hora te acostaste?

g) ¿Qué fue lo mejor?

h) ¿Con quién fuiste?

2. Gapped questions

a) ¿Qué vas a **hacer** el fin de semana **próximo**?   b) ¿Qué tiempo **hizo** el fin de **semana** pasado?

c) ¿Adónde **fuiste**? ¿Con **quién**?   d) ¿Cómo **fue**? ¿Qué fue lo **mejor**?   e) ¿A **qué** hora te **despertaste** el sábado pasado?

f) ¿A qué hora **vas a** levantarte el sábado **próximo**?   g) ¿Qué **hiciste** el domingo **pasado**?

3. Write the questions

a) ¿Adónde vas a ir?   b) ¿Con quién vas a ir?   c) ¿Qué vas a comprar?   d) ¿Cómo será?   e) ¿Con quién fuiste a la piscina?

f) ¿Cómo fue y qué fue lo mejor?   g) ¿Qué hicisteis luego?   h) ¿Qué tiempo hizo?

4. Break the flow

a) ¿A qué hora te acostaste?   b) ¿Qué hiciste el fin de semana pasado?   c) ¿Con quién vas a ir?   d) ¿Adónde fuiste?

e) ¿A qué hora te levantaste?   f) ¿Qué fue lo mejor?   g) ¿Qué tiempo hizo?   h) ¿Cómo lo pasaste?

i) ¿Qué vas a hacer el fin de semana próximo?

5. Spot and add in the one word missing

a) ¿Qué hiciste **el** fin de semana pasado?   b) ¿**A** qué hora te levantaste?   c) ¿Cómo **lo** pasaste?   d) ¿Qué tiempo **hizo**?

e) ¿Con quién fuiste **al** polideportivo?   f) ¿Adónde fuiste el fin **de** semana pasado?   g) ¿Adónde vas **a** ir el sábado próximo?

h) ¿Adónde vas a ir **el** domingo próximo?   i) ¿A qué hora **te** acostaste?

6. Complete the answers to the questions

Accept any suitable answers.

Unit 6: Talking about my daily routine & activities

1. Match

Tomo el desayuno – I have breakfast   **Hago mis deberes** – I do my homework   **Salgo de casa** – I leave my home

Me levanto – I get up   **Llego al colegio** – I arrive at school   **Me acuesto** – I go to bed   **Leo un libro** – I read a book

Me lavo la cara – I wash my face   **Me visto** – I get dressed   **Me ducho** – I shower   **Descanso** – I rest

Almuerzo – I have lunch   **Quiero** – I want   **Puedo** – I can

2. Missing letters

a) Tomo el desayuno   b) Descanso   c) Me lavo   d) Puedo   e) Quiero   f) Me levanto   g) Salgo de casa   h) Leo un libro

i) Llego al colegio   j) Me visto   k) Me ducho   l) Vuelvo **a** casa

3. Multiple choice

a) 3   b) 1   c) 2   d) 1   e) 3   f) 1   g) 2   h) 1   i) 2   j) 1

4. Complete with the missing verb

a) Me visto   b) Me lavo   c) Almuerzo   d) Leo un libro   e) Quiero   f) Voy a hacer   g) Debo   h) Me acuesto

5. Match action and place

Me lavo en el cuarto de baño ; **Almuerzo en** el restaurante ; **Me visto en** mi dormitorio ; **Hago footing en** el parque ;

Hago pesas en el gimnasio ; **Veo una película en** el cine ; **Voy de compras en** el centro comercial ;

Hago natación en la piscina

6. Arrange the actions in the correct chronological order

1 Me despierto ; 2 Me levanto ; 3 Tomo el desayuno ; 4 Voy al colegio ; 5 Llego al colegio ; 6 Almuerzo ; 7 Salgo del colegio ;

8 Ceno ; 9 Después de cenar, veo la tele

7. Faulty translation

a) I get up at 6:**30**   b) I shower **right away**   c) I **get dressed**   d) I **put on** my uniform   e) I **arrive at** school

f) I **go jogging**   g) I have **lunch**   h) I **leave from** school   i) I **rest**   j) I **go to bed**

8. Complete with the options below

a) Por lo general me levanto a las seis y **media**   b) Tomo el desayuno a eso de la siete menos **veinte**

c) Salgo de casa a eso de las siete y **diez** d) Cojo el autobús a las siete y **cuarto**   e) Llego al colegio a las ocho **menos** cuarto

f) Las clases empiezan a las ocho menos **cinco**   g) Almuerzo a **mediodía**

h) Vuelvo a casa en el autobús de las cuatro y **veinte**   i) Ceno a **eso** de las ocho de la tarde   j) Me acuesto a **medianoche**

9. Match

A las ocho y cuarto – 8: 15   **A las ocho y diez** – 8: 10   **A las ocho y media** – 8:30   **A las ocho y cinco** – 8:05

A las nueve menos cinco – 8:55   **A las nueve menos diez** – 8:50   **A las nueve menos cuarto** – 8:45

10. Sentence puzzle

a) Hoy no tengo que hacer mis deberes   b) Mañana no tengo que levantarme temprano

c) Esta tarde puedo salir con mis amigos   d) Mañana no tengo que ir al colegio   e) Este fin de semana voy a ir al estadio

f) El viernes próximo debo hacer las tareas   g) El sábado próximo puedo acostarme tarde

h) El domingo próximo puedo ir a la fiesta de Paco

11. Find someone who…

a) Susana   b) Pedro   c) Silvio   d) Ana Laura   e) Elena   f) Ana Laura   g) Pedro   h) Roberto   i) Gabriel

j) Marina   k) Carla

12. Gapped translation

a) Tomorrow I **can't** go out with my girlfriend because I have **a lot of homework**

b) Next **weekend** I am going to go to Amparo's **party**

c) Next **Sunday** I **want** to go to the beach

d) Today in the **afternoon/evening** I am going to go **shopping** with my mother

e) **Today** I don't want to do the chores. I am very **tired**

f) Every day, after **getting up** I **have to** make my bed

g) Today I **can't** go mountain biking because **the weather is bad**

h) Next **Saturday** I am not going to do anything. I am only going to **rest**

13. Sort the activities below in the appropriate box

Los deportes: a, h, k   **Las compras:** e, f, g   **Los estudios:** b, c, j   **Las tareas domésticas:** d, i, l

14. Complete with a suitable word

a) Hoy tengo que hacer mis **deberes**   b) Mañana quiero ir de **compras**   c) Esta tarde voy a ayudar a mi **padre/madre**

d) Esta mañana no voy a **ir** al colegio   e) Hoy quiero comer **pasta, etc.**   f) Tengo que **estudiar/revisar** para el examen

g) Quiero **montar** en bici   h) Llego al **colegio** a las ocho   i) Tomo el **desayuno** en la cocina   j) No hago **nada**

k) Leo un **libro** en mi habitación

15. Find the Spanish equivalent

a) temprano   b) debo coger   c) me ducho enseguida   d) tostadas con miel   e) después del desayuno   f) llego al

g) las clases empiezan   h) descanso un poco   i) no puedo salir   j) para mirar escaparates   k) voy a estudiar

16. Complete the sentences

a) During the week I get up **very early**   b) At 6:45 I must **catch the bus** to go to school)

c) For breakfast I have **toasts** with **honey**   d) After breakfast I put on the uniform and **leave from home** to catch the bus

e) Lessons start at **7:45** and end at **3:15**   f) At four I **go back home**   g) Before doing my homework I **take a shower and rest**

h) Today I must revise for my exams, so I **can't go out with my friends**

i) Between five and seven thirty we go to the shopping mall to **go window shopping** and to **go for a walk**

17. Find in the text

a) me levanto, me ducho   b) debo, tengo que   c) tostadas, miel   d) repasar, estudiar   e) salir, pasear, mirar escaparates

f) hoy   g) entre semana   h) hasta

18. Answer the questions in Spanish in full sentences, as if you were Eduardo

a) Por lo general me levanto a eso de las seis   b) Cojo el autobús a las siete menos cuarto

c) Desayuno unas tostadas con miel y zumo de naranja   d) Me pongo el uniforme después de desayunar

e) Las clases empiezan a las ocho menos cuarto   f) Porque hoy tengo que repasar para mis exámenes

g) Miramos escaparates y paseamos   h) Esta noche voy a estudiar hasta las once

19. Find the Spanish equivalent

a) entre semana   b) tengo que levantarme   c) enseguida   d) me cepillo los dientes   e) salgo de casa

f) llego al instituto   g) las clases empiezan   h) antes de salir del instituto   i) nos ayudamos   j) paso una hora

k) a causa de los exámenes   l) chismeamos   m) miramos escaparates

20. Translate into English

a) I usually get up quite early   b) I have to get up around half past six   c) Before leaving from home

d) Before leaving from school/highschool   e) We help each other when we don't understand something   f) I go back home

g) I rest a little before doing my homework   h) I can't go out with my friends nor chat with them

i) We go window shopping and buy clothes

21. Tick the phrases that you can find in Inés' text

a, d, f, h, k

22. Complete the text with one of the options below

Entre **semana** suelo levantarme bastante temprano. Tengo que **levantarme** a eso de las seis y media porque **debo** coger el autobús para el colegio a las siete y cuarto. Me ducho **enseguida** y después desayuno unas tostadas con **miel** y un zumo de manzana. Después del desayuno me cepillo los dientes y antes de **salir** de mi casa me pongo el uniforme. Luego salgo de casa **para** coger el autobús. Por lo general **llego** al colegio a eso de las ocho. Las clases empiezan a las ocho menos cuarto y **terminan** a las tres y cuarto. Antes **de** salir del colegio, por lo general, paso una hora o dos repasando en la **biblioteca**. Es bastante difícil y **aburrido**, pero mi **mejor** amiga Laura estudia conmigo, **así que** nos ayudamos cuando no comprendemos algo.

23. Jigsaw reading

3, 5, 1, 7, 4, 10, 2, 8, 6, 9, 11

24a. Translate the sentences into Spanish using *tengo que* + infinitive

a) Tengo que levantarme temprano   b) Tengo que hacer mis deberes   c) Tengo que ayudar a mi madre

d) Tengo que ir al colegio   e) Tengo que hacer mi cama   f) Tengo que acostarme temprano

g) Tengo que estudiar/revisar para los exámenes

24b. Translate the sentences into Spanish using *(no) puedo* + infinitive

a) Puedo salir con mis amigos   b) No puedo jugar en/con mi ordenador   c) Puedo montar en bici en el parque

d) Puedo acostarme tarde   e) No puedo tomar el desayuno / No puedo desayunar   f) Puedo ir al colegio en bici

g) Puedo levantarme temprano

24c. Translate the sentences into Spanish using *quiero / tengo que / puedo* + infinitive

a) Tengo que trabajar   b) No quiero ducharme   c) No puedo ir a la fiesta   d) Tengo que arreglar mi habitación

e) Quiero mirar la televisión   f) No quiero ir a pescar   g) No puedo levantarme temprano   h) Quiero comer pizza

i) No quiero jugar   j) Tengo que volver a casa   k) No quiero estudiar   l) Tengo que hacer mis deberes

25. Guided translation

a) **Mañana tengo** que **ir de compras** con mi madre   b) **Esta tarde no puedo salir** con mis amigos

c) **Hoy no puedo jugar** a los **videojuegos**   d) **Hoy no quiero hacer mis deberes**

e) **Este fin de semana quiero pasar tiempo** con mi **familia**   f) **Entre semana debo levantarme temprano**

g) **Esta mañana no puedo ir al colegio**   h) **Mañana no quiero ir a la fiesta**

* 26. Translate the following text into Spanish

Hola. Me llamo Marisa / Mi nombre es Marisa. Voy a hablarte/hablaros sobre mi rutina diaria.

Entre semana tengo que levantarme temprano porque debo coger el autobús para ir al colegio a las *seis y media. Me levanto a las seis y me ducho enseguida. Luego tomo el desayuno. Por lo general, como dos huevos, una tostada y un plátano. Después de desayunar salgo de casa y cojo el autobús para ir al colegio.

Normalmente llego al colegio a las siete y media. Las clases empiezan a las siete y cuarenta / ocho menos veinte y terminan a las dos y veinte. Mi asignatura favorita es español porque el profesor es muy bueno, guay y divertido.

Vuelvo a casa a las tres en punto. Después de volver/regresar descanso un poco, me ducho y luego tengo que hacer mis deberes o no puedo salir. A eso de las seis salgo con mis amigos. Normalmente vamos al centro comercial cerca de mi casa. Miramos escaparates, compramos ropa y chismorreamos sobre los chicos de nuestro colegio.

Debo volver a casa a las ocho para cenar. Después de cenar miro la televisión y luego me acuesto.

*original edition says "siete"

27. Write a 150 to 250 words paragraph

Accept any suitable answers.

Question Skills Unit 6

1. Split questions

¿**A qué** hora sales de casa?   ¿**Con** quién desayunas?   ¿**Dónde tomas el** desayuno?   ¿**Qué** desayunas normalmente?

¿**Qué haces** después del colegio?   ¿**Qué vas a** hacer el sábado próximo?   ¿**Te gusta** tu colegio?

¿**Cuál es** tu pasatiempo favorito?   ¿**Cómo** vas al colegio?   ¿**Por qué** te gusta?

2. Find and write in the missing words

a) Háblame de **tu** rutina diaria   b) ¿A qué hora **te** despiertas?   c) ¿**Con** quién desayunas?   d) ¿A qué **hora** sales de casa?

e) ¿Qué haces cuando vuelves **del** colegio?   f) ¿A **qué** hora haces tus deberes?   g) ¿Qué te gusta hacer **después** del colegio?

h) ¿Qué **vas** a hacer el fin de semana próximo?

3. Match questions and answers

¿**A qué hora te despiertas?** – Me despierto a las seis todos los días

¿**A qué hora te levantas?** – Me levanto a las siete

¿**Qué desayunas normalmente?** – Por lo general, una tostada con miel

¿**Con quién desayunas?** – Desayuno con mi madre

¿**Dónde tomas el desayuno?** – Suelo tomar el desayuno en la cocina

¿**A qué hora sales de casa?** – Salgo de casa a las ocho menos cuarto

¿**Cómo vas al colegio?** – A veces voy en coche y a veces en autobús

¿**Qué haces cuando vuelves del colegio?** – Cuando vuelvo a casa siempre leo un libro

¿**Qué tienes que hacer después del cole?** – Tengo que arreglar mi dormitorio, ¡qué aburrido!

¿**Qué te gusta hacer cuando vuelves del cole?** – Me gusta jugar a los videojuegos en línea

¿**Cuál es tu pasatiempo favorito?** – Mi pasatiempo favorito es tocar el ukelele

¿**Qué vas a hacer el fin de semana próximo?** – Voy a ir al centro comercial con mi novio

4. Guided translation

a) ¿Con quién desayunas?   b) ¿A qué hora te levantas?   c) ¿Cómo vas al colegio?   d) ¿Te gusta?

e) ¿Dónde tomas el desayuno?   f) ¿A qué hora te despiertas?   g) ¿Qué tareas tienes que hacer?

h) ¿Qué haces después del colegio?   i) ¿Cuál es tu pasatiempo favorito?

5. Translate into Spanish

a) ¿A qué hora te despiertas?   b) ¿A qué hora te levantas?   c) ¿Con quién desayunas/tomas el desayuno?

d) ¿Cómo vas al colegio?   e) ¿Te gusta?   f) ¿A qué hora vuelves a casa?   g) ¿Qué tareas tienes que hacer?

h) ¿Cuál es tu pasatiempo favorito?   i) ¿Qué vas a hacer el fin de semana próximo?

6. Answer the following questions in your own words, using full sentences

Accept any suitable answers.

Vocab Revision Workout 3

1. Translate into English

a) We are going to play basketball   b) My mother is going to go to the office   c) I am not going to go to school today

d) And you, what are you going to do tomorrow?   e) And you, what are you going to do today?

f) Tomorrow I am not going to study   g) My brother and I are going to play football

h) My siblings/brothers are going to go to the gym   i) My sister isn't going to do anything

j) This afternoon/evening my older brother is going to go clubbing

2. Complete with the correct form of the verb ir

a) voy   b) va   c) vamos   d) van   e) van   f) vamos   g) vas   h) vais   i) van

3. Gapped translation

a) La tienda de deporte está a**l lado** del cine   b) La piscina está **enfrente** del colegio

c) El centro comercial está al **final** de la calle   d) El banco está **detrás** de este edificio   e) El estadio está **lejos** de aquí

f) El supermercado está **cerca** de mi casa   g) Está **entre** la tienda y la piscina

4. Guided translation

a) Una s**illa bonita**   b) Una **cocina luminosa**   c) Una **alfombra roja**   d) Unas **cortinas azules**

e) Una h**abitación espaciosa**   f) Un **armario viejo**   g) Una **cama cómoda**   h) Un **edificio moderno**

i) Una **televisión nueva**   j) Un **barrio tranquilo**

5. Complete with a suitable word

a) En mi ciudad hay muchas **tiendas buenas**   b) Mi habitación favorita es **la cocina** porque es **luminosa**

c) Al lado del armario hay **el espejo**   d) El espejo **está** enfrente de la **cama**   e) En mi piso **hay** siete habitaciones

6. Faulty translation

a) In the kitchen there are four old **chairs**   b) In my **bedroom** there are red curtains   c) –

d) In our garden there **aren't any** trees   e) In our **living** room there are two armchairs

f) **Next to** my bed there is a bedside table   g) The mirror is near the **door**   h) –   i) In the kitchen there is a big **wardrobe**

7. Translate the sentences into Spanish using *quiero / debo / puedo* + infinitive

a) Debo estudiar   b) No quiero salir   c) No puedo ir a la fiesta   d) Debo arreglar la cocina   e) Quiero ver una película

f) Quiero ir al colegio   g) No puedo levantarme temprano   h) Quiero comer pasta   i) No quiero hacer footing

j) Debo ir al gimnasio   k) No quiero trabajar   l) Debo hacer mis deberes

8. Complete with the missing verbs

a) **Fui** a la tienda con mi padre   b) No **hice** nada el fin de semana pasado   c) Ayer por la tarde **vi** una película en el cine

d) **Monté** en bici en el centro   e) **Jugué** al tenis con mi padre   f) Me **relajé** escuchando música

g) Me **levanté** temprano para hacer footing con mi madre   h) **Fui** a una fiesta en casa de mi amiga Marta

i) **Saqué** muchas fotos   j) **Jugué** al baloncesto   k) **Me compré** un jersey   l) **Fui** al parque con mi novia

m) **Leí** tebeos en el salón

9. Translate into Spanish

a) En mi barrio hay muchas cosas que hacer para los jóvenes

b) El fin de semana pasado fui al centro comercial con mi madre

c) Hace tres días monté en mi bici y jugué con mis amigos en el parque

d) No quiero ir a la fiesta esta tarde

e) Nos relajamos escuchando música

f) Fuimos al casco antiguo y sacamos muchas fotos

g) La semana próxima vamos a ir a Madrid. Será divertido

h) Cada día ayudo a mi madre en la casa

i) Normalmente me levanto muy temprano por la mañana porque debo salir de casa para ir al colegio a las siete

j) Esta tarde no voy a hacer nada

Unit 7: Saying what I do to help at home – present & past

1. Match
Tengo que hacer la compra – I have to do the shopping
Tengo que lavar los platos – I have to wash the dishes
Suelo hacer la cama – I usually make the bed
Tengo que limpiar el suelo – I have to clean the floor
Tengo que poner la mesa – I have to lay the table
Suelo pasear al perro – I usually walk the dog
Suelo quitar la mesa – I usually clear the table
Suelo ayudar a mi hermano –I usually help my brother
Tengo que cortar el césped – I have to mow the lawn
Tengo que regar las plantas – I have to water the plants

2. Missing letters
a) Tengo que arreglar mi habitación   b) Suelo hacer la cama   c) Suelo limpiar el suelo   d) Tengo que regar las plantas
e) Suelo ayudar a mi hermano   f) Tengo que cocinar   g) Tengo que poner la mesa   h) Suelo quitar la mesa

3. Complete
a) Tengo que **arreglar** mi habitación   b) Suelo **ayudar** a mi hermano con sus deberes   c) Tengo que **cocinar**
d) Tengo que **regar** las plantas   e) Tengo que **cuidar** a mi hermana   f) Suelo h**acer** mi cama   g) Suelo **pasear** al perro
h) Tengo que **poner** y **quitar** la mesa

4. Give your opinion about the activities listed
Student's answers.

5. Write P for probable and I for improbable for the sentences below
a) I   b) I   c) P   d) I   e) P   f) P   g) P   h) I

6. Complete the table with the missing present forms of the verbs *poder*, *querer* and *tener que*

puedo	**quiero**	tengo que
puedes	quieres	tienes que
puede	**quiere**	**tiene que**
podemos	queremos	**tenemos que**
podéis	**queréis**	tenéis que
pueden	quieren	**tienen que**

7. Find in the text
a) somos cinco personas   b) todos tenemos que compartir las tareas   c) mi hermano mayor (también) tiene que hacer su cama
d) tengo que quitar la mesa   e) tiene que lavar el coche   f) tengo que ayudar a mi padre en el jardín
g) mi padre suele cocinar   h) y también tiene que cuidar el jardín   i) yo tengo que hacer mi cama   j) por supuesto
k) además   l) después del desayuno   m) lavar los platos   n) después de la cena   o) después del almuerzo

8. Translate into English
a) In my family we are six / there are six of us   b) My older brother is lazy   c) My younger brother is hardworking
d) My mother has to work in the garden   e) My father has to cook   f) I have to make my bed   g) I usually also wash the car
h) Moreover, I usually lay the table   i) My younger brother usually washes the dishes
j) Also, he usually helps my father in the garden   k) My older brother doesn't want to do anything
l) He has to make his bed, but he never does it

 **THE LANGUAGE GYM**

9. Sentence puzzle

a) Dos días por semana tengo que lavar el coche de mi padre

b) Una vez por semana tengo que ayudar a mi padre en el jardín

c) Todos los días tengo que hacer mi cama y pasear al perro

d) Todos los sábados tengo que cortar el césped, pero el sábado pasado no lo hice

e) Después del almuerzo suelo quitar la mesa, pero hoy no pude porque tenía muchos deberes

f) Después de levantarme suelo hacer mi cama, pero hoy no pude

g) Todos los días suelo ayudar a mi hermano con sus deberes, pero ayer no quise

10. Rock climbing translation

a) Hoy tengo que lavar las plantas después del almuerzo   b) Esta tarde tengo que pasear al perro

c) Después de levantarme tengo que hacer mi cama   d) Todos los días tengo que poner y quitar la mesa

e) Los sábados suelo lavar el coche de mi padre

11. Complete with the missing letters

a) No hice **nada**   b) No **paseé** al perro   c) No **hice** la cama   d) No limpié el **suelo**   e) No **pude**   f) No **qu**ise **ayudar**

g) No **limpié** los platos   h) No q**uité** la mesa   i) No **ayudé** a mis padres   j) No **cociné**

12. Faulty translation

a) I **vacuum cleaned**   b) I didn't **do** anything   c) I didn't **clear** the table   d) I didn't **wash the dishes**

e) I **tidied up** my room   f) I **washed** the dishes   g) I didn't **lay** the table   h) I **made** the bed   i) I **walked** the dog

13. Spot and correct the errors

a) No pas**é** la aspiradora   b) No puse la mesa   c) –   d) **No** hice nada   e) Quité **la** mesa   f) No ayudé **a** mi padre

g) Hice **la** compra

14. Tangled translation: rewrite in Spanish

a) Todos los **días** suelo pasear al **perro**, pero ayer **no pude**

b) El **sábado** tengo que **lavar el coche pero** el sábado **pasado no quise**

c) Después del desayuno **suelo** quitar la **mesa** pero ayer no lo **hice**

d) Anteayer **arreglé** mi habitación y **lavé** los platos pero ayer no hice **nada**

e) Todos **los días** tengo que hacer mi **cama**, sin embargo esta **mañana** no **quise**

f) El domingo suelo **ayudar** a mi **hermano** con sus **deberes**, **sin embargo** el domingo **pasado** no lo hice

g) Todos los **viernes** suelo **ir al** supermercado **con** mi madre, pero el **viernes** pasado no **fui** con **ella** porque estaba **cansada/o**

15. Complete with a suitable word based on the HELP BOX

a) Ayer no **tenía** ganas   b) Me **dolía** la cabeza   c) **Estaba** ocupado   d) **No** pude   e) **Me** dolía la espalda

f) **Tenía** muchos deberes que hacer   g) No **pude**   h) Me dolía la **cabeza**   i) Me dolía **el** brazo   j) No **me** acordé

16. Multiple choice

a) 2   b) 3   c) 2   d) 2   e) 3   f) 1   g) 3   h) 2   i) 1   j) 3

17. Translate into English

a) Yesterday I didn't walk the dog because I was ill

b) The day before yesterday I didn't wash the dishes because I didn't feel like it

c) This morning I didn't go to school because my head hurt

d) This afternoon/evening I didn't take out the rubbish because my arm hurt a lot

e) Last weekend I didn't wash the car because my back hurt a lot

f) Last Sunday I didn't do anything to help at home because I was very busy

g) Last weekend I didn't help my parent because I was angry with them

h) Every day I lay and clear the table, but yesterday I didn't want to because I didn't feel like it

 **THE LANGUAGE GYM**

18. Wordsearch

a) Suelo ayudar

b) Estaba ocupado

c) No tenía ganas

d) No pude

e) No hice la cama

f) No hice nada

g) No ayudé a mi padre

h) Me dolía la cabeza

i) No puse la mesa

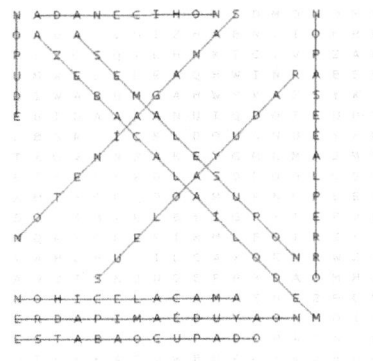

19. Match

No pude – I wasn't able to   **No ayudé a mi padre** – I didn't help my father   **No tenía ganas** – I didn't feel like it

Estaba ocupado – I was busy   **No puse la mesa** – I didn't lay the table   **No hice nada** – I didn't do anything

Me dolía el brazo – My arm hurt   **Me dolía la cabeza** – My head hurt   **Suelo lavar el coche** – I usually wash the car

No paseé al perro – I didn't walk the dog   **No lavé los platos** – I didn't wash the dishes

No lavé el coche – I didn't wash the car   **Tengo que poner la mesa** – I have to lay the table

Estaba enfadada – I was angry   **No quise** – I didn't want to

20. Missing letters

a) No puse la mesa porque no tenía ganas   b) No paseé a mi perro porque estaba enferma

c) No hice nada porque estaba cansado   d) No ayudé a mi padre porque no quise

e) No hice la compra con mi madre porque estaba enfadada con ella   f) No quité la mesa porque estaba ocupado

g) No jugué con mi hermano porque no pude   h) Ayer no cociné porque me dolía la cabeza   i) Ayer no lavé el coche

21. Find in the text

a) hay mucho que hacer para los jóvenes   b) soy muy deportista   c) en mi tiempo libre   d) escalada

e) estos deportes   f) siempre compartimos las tareas   g) suele cocinar   h) cuidar el jardín

i) pasear al perro   j) hacer la cama   k) arreglar nuestra habitación   l) sacar la basura   m) están muy contentos

22. Gapped translation

My name is Pablo. I am **thirteen** years old and am from Buenos Aires in Argentina. In my city there is a lot to do **for young people**. There are many **sport facilities**, which is very important **for me** because I am very **sporty**. In my **free time** I go swimming, **rock climbing** and cycling. I love these sports. In my city there are also lots of **shops** that I **like** and some really good bars and restaurants.

In my family we always **share** the **chores**. My mother usually **cooks** and looks after **the garden**. My father has to **wash the car** and **walk** the **dog**. My brother and I have to **make** the **bed**, tidy **our room**, take out **the rubbish** and **lay** and **clear** the **table**. Our parents are very happy when we **help them**. However, yesterday I couldn't because I was **sick**.

23. Answer the following questions in Spanish, as if you were Pablo

a) Soy de Buenos Aires   b) En mi tiempo libre hago natación, escalada y ciclismo

c) En mi ciudad hay muchas instalaciones deportivas   d) Mi padre lava el coche y pasea el perro

e) Mi madre suele cocinar y cuidar el jardín   f) Hago la cama, arreglo la habitación, saco la basura y pongo y quito la mesa

g) Mi hermano hace las mismas tareas que yo

24. Tick the items below which are contained in Pablo's text and cross out the ones which aren't

a) **me encantan**

b) **contentos**

c) barrio

d) **ayudamos**

e) vamos

f) **tenemos que**

g) planchar

h) **lavar**

i) hermana

j) **sin embargo**

k) **deportista**

l) trabajar

m) **cuidar**

n) se puede

25. True, False or Not mentioned?

a) True   b) False   c) False   d) Not mentioned   e) False   f) True   g) False   h) False   i) True

26. Who does what?

a) The older brother   b) The older brother   c) The mother   d) The older brother, the sister and Miguel

e) The mother, and the older brother helps her   f) Miguel   g) The father   h) The sister   i) The older brother   j) Miguel

27. Find in Miguel's text the Spanish equivalent for the following items

a) afueras   b) no hay   c) luminosa   d) acogedora   e) hermoso   f) escritorio   g) todos compartimos   h) tareas   i) justo

j) nuestras   k) ayudar   l) lavar   m) no pudo   n) plancho la ropa   o) enfadada   p) quito la mesa   q) plancho la ropa

r) ayudo a mi hermana   s) sin embargo   t) no tenía ganas

28. Complete

a) **Suelo pasear al perro**   b) **Tengo que poner la mesa**   c) **No hice nada**   d) **Mi hermano tiene que cocinar**

e) **Tengo que lavar la ropa**   f) **Mi hermano mayor suele sacar la basura**   g) **Ayer no quise ayudar a mis padres**

h) **Suelo ayudar a mi hermano, pero ayer no pude**   i) **Todos compartimos las tareas domésticas**

29. Write two paragraphs for Jordi in the first person singular (*yo*) and for Carolina in the third person singular (*ella*)

Jordi: Me llamo Jordi y tengo trece años. Mi barrio está en las afueras de la ciudad y es muy feo porque hay muchas fábricas. No hay mucho que hacer en mi barrio. Hay un estadio, pero no hay muchas instalaciones deportivas. El fin de semana monto en bici en el parque, voy a la casa de mi amigo y también voy al cine con mi familia.

El fin de semana pasado fui a la fiesta de Paco, hice mucho deporte y me relajé escuchando música y mirando la televisión. Para ayudar en casa, suelo poner y quitar la mesa. También tengo que hacer mi cama, arreglar mi habitación y ayudar a mi padre en el jardín, pero ayer no pude ayudar a mi padre porque estaba enfermo.

Carolina: Ella se llama Carolina y tiene diecisiete años. Vive en el centro de la ciudad, en un barrio histórico muy bonito. En su barrio hay mucho que hacer para los jóvenes, hay muchas áreas verdes y muchas instalaciones deportivas. El fin de semana Carolina va a mirar escaparates, sale con sus amigas y va de marcha.

El fin de semana pasado hizo turismo y sacó muchas fotos. También fue de compras y visitó a sus primos. Normalmente, para ayudar en casa Carolina prepara la comida y lava el coche de su madre. También tiene que hacer su cama y cuidar a su hermano menor. Sin embargo, ayer no pudo lavar el coche de su madre porque estaba ocupada.

 **THE LANGUAGE GYM**

Question Skills Unit 7

1. Sentence puzzle
a) ¿Qué tareas no te gusta hacer?   b) ¿Quién corta el césped?   c) ¿Qué hiciste ayer para ayudar a tus padres?

d) ¿Quién cocina en tu familia normalmente?   e) ¿Con qué frecuencia ayudas a tus padres?   f) ¿Cuándo ayudas en casa?

g) ¿Quién lava el coche de tu padre?   h) ¿Por qué no ayudaste en casa ayer?   i) ¿Qué tareas hiciste el fin de semana pasado?

2. Match the sentences below with the questions in Exercise 1
a) c   b) d   c) b   d) e   e) a   f) h   g) g   h) i   i) f

3. Answer the questions below as if you were Domingo
a) Todos compartimos las tareas domésticas

b) Tenemos que hacer nuestras camas y arreglar nuestras habitaciones todos los días

c) Mi padre saca la basura y cuida el jardín   d) Ayuda a mi padre

e) David lava el coche de mis padres una vez por semana   f) Porque estaba enfadado

g) Ayuda a nuestro hermano menor con sus deberes   h) Con los deberes de ciencias y matemáticas

i) Mi tía Denisse   j) Porque estaba enferma

4. Translate into English
a) Tell me about your daily routine   b) What do you do to help at home?   c) How often do you help with the chores?

d) Who cooks in your home?   e) Who tidies your room?   f) What chores do you hate doing? Why?

g) What do your siblings do to help at home?   h) What did you do to help at home last weekend?

i) Why did you not help your parents yesterday?   j) Who was sick yesterday?

k) At what time did you do the dishes yesterday?   l) What did your mother cook last Sunday?

m) Who helped your father in the garden?

5. Complete with the missing words
a) ¿**Cómo** te llamas?

b) ¿Cuántos **años** tienes?

c) ¿**Dónde** vives?

d) ¿Con **quién** vives?

e) ¿En qué parte de la **ciudad** vives?

f) ¿Cómo **es** tu barrio?

g) ¿Qué se puede **hacer** en tu barrio?

h) ¿**Hay** tiendas buenas?

i) ¿Qué instalaciones **deportivas** hay?

j) ¿**Qué** hiciste en tu barrio ayer?

k) ¿Cómo fue? ¿Qué fue lo **mejor**?

l) ¿Qué **vas** a hacer el fin de semana próximo?

m) ¿Qué haces normalmente para **ayudar** en casa?

n) ¿Qué **tarea** no te gusta hacer?

Unit 8: Describing a typical day at school

1. Match

Llego al colegio – I arrive at school   **Salgo del colegio** – I leave school   **Hago mis deberes** – I do my homework
Voy a la biblioteca – I go to the library   **Voy a la cantina** – I go to the canteen   **Como en la cantina** – I eat in the canteen
El recreo es a mediodía – Break is at noon   **Tengo la última clase** – I have the last lesson   **Tengo inglés** – I have English
Escucho al profe – I listen to the teacher   **Tengo historia** – I have history
Charlo con mis compañeros – I chat with my schoolmates

2. Missing letters

a) La tercera clase   b) La primera clase   c) Llego al colegio   d) Salgo del colegio   e) Hago mis deberes
f) Escucho al profe   g) Charlo con mis compañeros   h) Como en la cantina   i) Hago cola en la cantina
j) Hay una pausa para comer

3. Complete with the missing words

a) Por lo general llego al colegio a las ocho y cuarto   b) El lunes, mi primera clase es español   c) Después tenemos el recreo
d) Durante el recreo charlo con mis amigos   e) Luego tengo la segunda clase, que es la clase de historia
f) No me gusta la historia porque es muy aburrida   g) Luego, es la hora de comer   h) Tengo que hacer cola en la cantina
i) Suelo comer pasta o arroz con pollo o carne   j) Mi última clase es a las dos y media

4. Put the actions below in chronological order

5, 6, 9, 1, 10, 7, 2, 11, 3, 8, 12, 4

5. Spot and correct the grammar/spelling mistakes

a) Voy al club de ajedrez   g) No puedo llevar faldas cortas
b) Llego al colegio a las ocho   h) No debo llevar pendientes
c) Tengo la clase de historia   i) No se puede masticar chicle
d) Durante el recreo   j) Tengo mi última clase
e) Salgo del colegio   k) Mi segunda clase es inglés
f) Voy a la biblioteca   l) Las clases terminan a las tres

6. Gapped translation

a) In my school one cannot **smoke**   b) My **first** class is English
c) On Fridays my first class is **IT (Information Technology)**   d) Break is at **half past nine**
e) During break I play **basketball**   f) In my school one cannot wear **earrings**   g) I usually do my homework in the **library**
h) You must **queue** in the canteen   i) One cannot eat in the **classrooms**   j) I have to wear a **school uniform**

7. Which of the following are unlikely to be REAL school rules?

a) probable   b) improbable   c) probable   d) improbable   e) improbable   f) improbable   g) improbable
h) improbable   i) improbable   j) probable   k) improbable

8. Sentence puzzle

a) No se puede fumar   b) Se debe llevar uniforme   c) Tengo que hacer cola en la cantina   d) No se puede utilizar el móvil
e) Tienes que hacer los deberes   f) Las clases empiezan a las ocho y cuarto   g) No se puede masticar chicle
h) No se puede llevar pendientes   i) Se debe respetar a los profesores   j) Se debe levantar la mano antes de hablar

9. Complete with a suitable word

a) No se puede **fumar** cigarrillos   h) Se debe **respetar** a los profesores
b) Las clases **terminan** a las tres y media   i) Se debe **hacer** los deberes
c) Vuelvo a **casa** en autobús   j) No se puede **mirar/utilizar** el móvil
d) A la hora de **comer** no como mucho   k) Las clases **empiezan** a las ocho
e) Se debe **hacer** cola en la cantina   l) Voy al colegio **a pie**
f) Hago mis deberes en la **biblioteca**   m) No se puede **masticar** chicle
g) No se puede llevar **maquillaje/pendientes**   n. Se debe **llevar** uniforme

10. Translate into English

a) My first lesson is English   b) My favorite subject is Spanish   c) I can't stand German   d) IT is an exciting subject

e) Sciences are very boring   f) I love my English lessons   g) On Monday, my last lesson is PE

h) My Math teacher is too strict   i) In the Music lesson one must work a lot   j) The Technology teacher is very good

k) The French teacher is very funny and cool

11. Faulty translation

a) One must not **chat** in lessons   b) One cannot wear **earrings**   c) One must raise their hand before **speaking**

d) One cannot **chew gum**   e) One cannot **smoke** in the corridors   f) One cannot wear **trainers**

g) One cannot wear **make up**   h) One must **listen to** the teachers

12. Complete with *puedo* or *puede* as appropriate

a) No se **puede** fumar   b) No se **puede** correr en los pasillos   c) No se **puede** llevar faldas cortas

d) Yo no **puedo** llevar maquillaje   e) Yo no **puedo** utilizar mi móvil   f) No se **puede** masticar chicle

g) No se **puede** llevar pendientes   h) Yo **puedo** jugar al baloncesto durante el recreo

i) No se **puede** hablar sin levantar la mano

13. Split sentences

No se puede llevar pendientes   **No puedo utilizar el** móvil   **No se puede correr en** los pasillos

Se debe levantar la mano antes de hablar   **Tengo que hacer** cola en la cantina   **Las clases empiezan** a las ocho

En el recreo suelo jugar al baloncesto   **A última hora tengo** matemáticas   **Me encanta la** profe de historia

14. Gapped translation

a) No se debe **comer** en clase   b) No se puede **llevar** pendientes   c) Se debe **levantar** la mano antes de hablar

d) No se puede **masticar** chicle   e) No se puede **correr** en los pasillos   f) No se puede **llevar** zapatillas de deporte

g) No se puede **llevar** maquillaje   h) Se debe **respetar** las reglas   i) Se debe **escuchar** a los profesores

15. Read the box on the left and find someone who, in their school...

a) Marta   b) Sonia   c) Susana   d) Marcelo   e) Marina   f) José   g) Juan   h) Conchi   i) Susana   j) José   k) Conchi

l) María

16. Wordsearch

a) No puedo

b) Llevar maquillaje

c) Masticar chicle

d) Voy al colegio

e) No debo

f) Fumar

g) No se puede

h) Llevar faldas cortas

i) No se debe

17. Complete the two texts with the options below

a. Voy a hablarte de un **día** escolar típico en mi colegio. Voy a un colegio en Londres, en Inglaterra. Las **clases** empiezan a las ocho y cuarto. El lunes, mi **primera** clase es dibujo. Me encanta el dibujo porque el profe es bueno y muy **divertido** Luego tenemos el **recreo** hasta la nueve y media. Durante el recreo juego al **fútbol** con mis amigos. Luego tengo español. Me encantan las clases de español porque son **divertidas** y aprendo mucho. La hora de comer **es** a la una menos cuarto. La **última** clase empieza a las dos menos diez. Por lo general, **salgo** del colegio a eso de las tres y media, después del club de **ajedrez**. Me **encanta** mi colegio.

b. Voy a **hablarte** de un día escolar típico en mi colegio. Voy a una escuela internacional en Buenos Aires. Las clases **empiezan** a las ocho menos veinte. El **lunes** a primera hora tengo ciencias. Luego **tengo** geografía. No me gusta esta **asignatura** porque es aburrida. Además, el profe es muy **estricto**. El recreo empieza a las nueve y veinticinco y **termina** a las diez menos veinticinco. Luego tengo matemáticas hasta **mediodía**. A la hora del almuerzo como y **charlo** con mis compañeros de clase en la cantina. Por lo general, como pollo con **arroz** o pasta. La última clase empieza a la una y diez. No me gusta **mucho** mi colegio. Odio **estudiar**, aunque sé que es muy importante.

18. Find the Spanish equivalent

a) llego al colegio   b) las clases empiezan   c) nunca hacemos trabajo de grupo   d) durante el recreo

e) tengo inglés   f) es la hora de comer   g) comemos y charlamos   h) comí arroz   i) soy muy deportista

j) las reglas son bastante estrictas

19. Correct the statements

a) Guillermo **can't stand** geography   b) **During break** he plays basketball   c) He learns **a lot** in the Spanish lessons

d) The English teacher shouts **a lot**   e) **Last** Monday he **ate** rice with chicken   f) He **loves** sport

g) There are **35** grams of sugar in a Coke   h) **Last** Friday he **had to** tidy up the headteacher's office

20. Correct the mistakes in these sentences from Guillermo's text and then translate them

a) Llego al colegio a eso **de** las ocho. *I get to school at around eight*

b) Durante el recreo juego **al** baloncesto. *During break I play basketball*

c) *Nunca hacemos trabaj**o** de grupo. *We never do group work*

d) Comemos y charlamos. *We eat and chat*

e) Me encanta porque soy muy **deportista**. *I love it because I am very sporty*

f) No se puede utilizar **el** móvil. *One cannot use the mobile phone*

g) No se puede correr en los **pasillos**. *One cannot run in the halls*

h) Se debe hacer **los** deberes. *One must do the homework*

i) Si se romp**en** las reglas. *If the rules are broken*

j) Tuve **que** pasar un**a** hora con el director. *I had to spend one hour with the headteacher*

k) Fue aburridísimo. *It was very boring*

Earliest edition – c) has no error

21. Answer the following questions

a) at around 8   b) at 8.15   c) he plays basketball with his friends   d) very fun   e) a lot!

f) the teacher shouts a lot and is too strict   g) rice with chicken   h) because he is very sporty

i) one must wear the uniform, one cannot use the mobile phone, one cannot smoke, one must do the homework every day

j) the punishments are very harsh   k) he didn't do his homework

l) he had to spend one hour with the headteacher tidying up his office, it was very boring

22. Complete the sentences below based on the text

a) school day   b) 8.30   c) History   d) unfriendly / fun   e) break   f) jokes   g) shouts / explain   h) football / yard   i) chat
j) meat with potatoes / orange juice   k) last / friendly

23. Find in the last paragraph of Adriana's text the Spanish equivalent of the following items

a) hay demasiadas reglas   b) se debe llevar   c) no se puede utilizar   d) no se puede fumar   e) no se puede correr

f) antes de hablar   g) los castigos   h) tuve que pasar una hora

24. Correct the false statements

a) Adriana come algo en la cantina durante el recreo   b) A Adriana le encanta francés   c) La profe de dibujo grita mucho

d) Adriana come carne   e) La clase favorita de Adriana es ciencias   f) En su colegio hay demasiadas reglas

g) El miércoles pasado Adriana llegó tarde

25. Translate the last paragraph of Adriana's text into English

In my school there are too many strict rules. One must wear uniform; one cannot use the mobile phone; one cannot smoke; one cannot run in the halls; one cannot use the lift; one must do the homework every day and one must always raise the hand before speaking in class. If one breaks the rules / If the rules are broken the punishments are very harsh. Last Wednesday I arrived late at school and I had to spend one hour with the headteacher cleaning his office. It was very boring!

26. Match questions and answers

¿**Cómo vas al colegio?** – Voy en bici

¿**A qué hora llegas?** – A eso de las ocho menos cuarto de la mañana

¿**Cuál es tu primera clase el viernes?** – A primera hora tengo dibujo

¿**Por qué no te gusta el profe de historia?** – Porque es muy antipático y me chilla

¿**Quién es tu profe preferido?** – La profesora de español

¿**Por qué?** – Porque siempre me ayuda

¿**Qué haces durante el recreo?** – Como y charlo con mis amigos en la cantina

¿**Hacéis deporte en tu colegio?** – Sí, hacemos atletismo y natación

¿**A qué hora vuelves a casa?** ¿**Cómo?** – A eso de las tres y media de la tarde, en autobús

¿**Cómo son las reglas en tu colegio?** – Son muy estrictas. No me gustan

¿**Cuál es la regla que menos te gusta?** – Que no se puede llevar maquillaje

27. Translate into Spanish

a) **Llego al colegio a eso de las ocho**   b) **Hoy mi primera clase es inglés**   c) **Luego tengo español**

d) **La hora de comer es a mediodía**   e) **Mi última clase es informática**   f) **Odio esta asignatura**

g) **En mi colegio hay muchas reglas**   h) **No se puede llevar maquillaje**

28a. Translate the two paragraphs into Spanish

1. Suelo llegar al colegio a las ocho y cuarto. Los lunes mi primera clase es historia. Me encanta historia porque el profesor es simpático y divertido. Entonces tengo el recreo hasta las nueve y media. Durante el recreo suelo hablar con mi mejor amigo Paco o con mi novia. Mi segunda clase es inglés. No me gusta esta asignatura. El almuerzo es a mediodía. Después del almuerzo tengo dos clases más: inglés y matemáticas. No me gustan estas asignaturas porque son demasiado difíciles. En mi colegio las reglas son muy estrictas. No se puede correr en los pasillos; no se puede llevar maquillaje o pendientes; no se puede utilizar el ascensor; no se puede hablar sin levantar la mano y las chicas no pueden llevar maquillaje.

2. Las reglas de mi colegio son muy estrictas. En primer lugar, se debe llegar a las siete cuarenta y cinco en punto. En segundo lugar, se debe llevar un uniforme. Lo odio, porque no puedo llevar mi gorra de béisbol y zapatillas deportivas favoritas. También, no puedo masticar chicle ni utilizar mi móvil. Tampoco puedo jugar a videojuegos durante el recreo y la pausa del almuerzo. En clase, no se puede hablar sin levantar la mano y no se puede ir al baño. Lo que me gusta de mi colegio, sin embargo, es que los profesores son amables. Aprendo mucho y se puede hacer mucho deporte.

28b. Write a 150-250 words text about a typical school day of yours, listing five key rules

Accept any suitable answers.

Question Skills Unit 8

1. Complete with the missing words

a) ¿A **qué** hora te levantas por lo general?   f) ¿Qué no se puede **hacer** en tu colegio?

b) ¿A qué hora **empiezan** las clases?   g) ¿Quién **es** tu profesora favorita?

c) ¿**Cuántas** clases tienes al día?   h) ¿A qué **hora** sales del colegio?

d) ¿**Cuál** es tu asignatura favorita?   i) ¿Qué actividades extraescolares **hay**?

e) ¿Se **puede** llevar maquillaje?   j) ¿**Cómo** es un día escolar típico?

2. Write the questions to the answers

a) ¿A qué hora empiezan las clases?   b) ¿Cuántas clases tienes?   c) ¿Qué asignatura te gusta más y por qué?

d) ¿Cuál es tu asignatura favorita?   e) ¿Qué asignatura no soportas?   f) ¿Quién es tu profesor favorito? ¿Por qué?

g) ¿Qué no se puede hacer en tu colegio?   h) ¿Se puede llevar maquillaje?   i) ¿Cómo son las reglas?

3. Guided translation

a) ¿A qué hora terminan las clases?   b) ¿Cómo son las reglas del colegio?   c) ¿Cuál es tu clase favorita?

d) ¿Se puede llevar maquillaje?   e) ¿Cuántas clases tienes al día?   f) ¿Cómo es un día escolar típico?

g) ¿Se puede fumar?   h) ¿Se puede llevar faldas cortas?

 **THE LANGUAGE GYM**

4. Spot and correct the errors in the sentences below

a) ¿Como **es** un día escolar típico en tu colegio?   b) ¿Cuántas clase**s** tienes al día?   c) ¿A qu**é** hora empieza**n** las clases?

d) ¿Se puede llevar faldas **cortas**?   e) ¿Se puede utiliz**ar** el móvil?   f) ¿Cuál **es** tu asignatura favorita?

g) ¿**Qué** actividades extraescolares hay?   h) ¿Quién **es** tu profesor favorito?   i) ¿Qué **se** debe llevar en tu colegio?

j) ¿A qué hora termina**n** las clases?   k) ¿Por qué no te gusta**n** las ciencias?

5. Translate into Spanish

a) ¿Cuántas clases tienes?   b) ¿Cuál es tu clase favorita?   c) ¿Por qué no te gustan las matemáticas?

d) ¿Quién es tu profesor/a favorito/a?   e) ¿Qué asignaturas no te gustan?   f) ¿A qué hora empiezan y terminan las clases?

g) ¿Cómo es un día escolar típico?   h) ¿Qué no se puede hacer en tu colegio?   i) ¿Se puede fumar?

j) ¿Se puede utilizar el móvil?   k) ¿Qué se debe hacer?   l) ¿Se debe hacer cola en la cantina?

Vocab Revision Workout 4

1. Match

Tengo que quitar la mesa – I have to clear the table   **Tengo que lavar el coche** – I have to wash the car

Suelo hacer la cama – I usually make the bed   **Tengo que limpiar el suelo** – I have to clean the floor

Tengo que poner la mesa – I have to lay the table   **Suelo pasear al perro** – I usually walk the dog

Suelo quitar la mesa – I usually clear the table   **Suelo ayudar a mi hermano** – I usually help my brother

Tengo que cocinar – I have to cook   **Tengo que regar las plantas** – I have to water the plants

2. Translate the sentences below into Spanish using *(No) Puedo + infinitive*

a) No puedo salir con mis amigas   b) No puedo jugar en mi ordenador   c) Puedo montar en bici en el parque

d) Puedo acostarme tarde   e) No puedo desayunar   f) Puedo ir al colegio en bici

3. Split sentences

Comí carne y ensalada   **Me relajé** leyendo   **No hice** nada   **Compré** un vestido rosa   **Vi** un partido de fútbol en la tele

Fui al centro comercial   **Hice ciclismo** de montaña   **Me levanté** tempramo   **Monté** en bici   **Jugué** al baloncesto

4. Sentence puzzle

a) El fin de semana pasado fuimos al cine juntos   b) Ayer me levanté temprano y saqué muchas fotos

c) Me relajé escuchando música antes de acostarme   d) Hicimos ciclismo de montaña en el campo

e) El domingo hicimos senderismo en las colinas

5. Translate into English

a) I went to the swimming pool   b) I am going to go shopping   c) We went to the countryside

d) We did sport   e) We are going to ride the bike   f) I went swimming   g) I am going to go to the stadium

h) Yesterday we played basketball   i) We went sightseeing   j) We saw cartoons   k) I went for a walk in the park

6. Complete the table below with the missing verb forms

1) Fuimos de compras   2) Hice mis deberes   3) Hago mis deberes   4) Voy a montar en bici   5) Fui al estadio

6) Voy a ir al estadio   7) Monté a caballo   8) Voy a montar a caballo   9) Voy a ir a una fiesta   10) Fui a la piscina

11) Voy a la piscina   12) Monté en monopatín   13) Vi una película   14) Voy a ver una película   15) Veo dibujos animados

16) Voy a ver dibujos animados

7. Faulty translation

a) Tomorrow I am going to **stay home**   b) Next **Saturday** I am going to watch a film

c) Next Thursday we are going to **ride the bike**   d) This Sunday **afternoon** I am going to go shopping

e) On Friday my parents are going to **rest**   f) Next week**end**   g) My **sister** is going to go to the **swimming pool**

h) In the **afternoon** I am going to do my homework

8. Complete with the missing letters

a) En mi b**arrio**   b) Se p**uede** c**omer** b**ien**   c) Se p**uede** i**r** de c**ompras**   d) Se p**uede** h**acer** d**eporte**

e) Se p**uede** m**ontar** e**n** b**ici**   f) A**yer** f**uimos** al c**ine**   g) A**nteayer** f**ui** al e**stadio**   h) V**i** u**na** p**elícula** b**uena**

Unit 9: Making after-school plans with a friend

1. Match
Dar una vuelta en bici – To go for a bike ride **Jugar al baloncesto** – To play basketball
Ver una película – To watch a film **Ir al estadio** – To go to the stadium **No hacer nada** – To not do anything
Hacer pesas – To do weights **Hacer natación** – To do swimming **Salir con mi novia** – To go out with my girlfriend
Quedarme en casa – To stay at home **Salir con mi mejor amigo** – To go out with my best friend **Estudiar** – To study
Ir a la casa de un amigo – To go to a friend's house **Meterme en Internet** – To go on the Internet

2. Complete with the appropriate option
a) Quiero **dar** una vuelta en bici b) No quiero **hacer** nada c) Me gustaría **salir** con mis amigos
d) Tengo que **fregar** el suelo ahora e) Tenemos que **lavar** el coche de papá f) Queremos **ir** a la casa de Felipe
g) Nos gustaría **ver** una película en el cine h) Quiero **ayudar** a mi madre con las tareas

3. Sort the sentences in the categories below
Tareas domésticas: 3, 11, 14, 16 **Pasatiempos:** 1, 5, 6, 7, 8, 13, 15 **Trabajo escolar:** 2, 4, 9, 10, 12

4. Sentence puzzle
a) ¿A qué hora quedamos? b) Esta tarde quiero ir al cine c) Quedamos enfrente del cine
d) No me apetece ir a la casa de Paco hoy e) ¿Qué quieres hacer hoy? f) No puedo salir contigo hoy
g) Tengo que ayudar a mi madre h) Me apetece ir al cine contigo

5. Translate into English
a) I fancy going for a bice ride this afternoon/evening b) I want to go to the stadium with my father tomorrow
c) Today I have to study before going out with my boyfriend d) I don't fancy / I don't feel like doing sport today
e) I want to play chess with my brother f) I have to revise for my Math exam g) We have to help our mother today

6. Multiple choice
a) 3 b) 3 c) 1 d) 3 e) 2 f) 1 g) 2 h) 2 i) 1 j) 3

7. Match
¿Qué tal? – How are you?
¿Qué quieres hacer esta tarde? – What do you want to do this evening?
¿Te apetece? – Do you fancy it?
¿Dónde quedamos? – Where shall we meet?
¿A qué hora quedamos? – At what time shall we meet?
¿Con quién vamos? – Who are we going with?
¿Por qué no puedes venir? – Why can't you come?
¿Qué vamos a hacer? – What are we going to do?

8. Match questions and answers
¿Qué tal? – Estoy muy bien, gracias
¿Qué quieres hacer esta tarde? – Quiero ir al parque
¿Te apetece? – No, no tengo ganas, prefiero ir al cine
¿Dónde quedamos? – Enfrente de la parada del autobús
¿A qué hora quedamos? – A las siete y media
¿Con quién vamos? – Con Pablo y Miguel
¿Por qué no puedes venir? – Porque tengo que estudiar para el examen
¿Qué vamos a hacer? – Vamos a jugar a la Play y escuchar música

9. Complete with the missing letters
a) H**ola** b) ¿D**ónde**? c) Me a**petece** d) **Tengo** que e) Nos **vemos** f) **Luego** g) Lo **siento** h) No **puedo**
i) Me **gustaría** j) No q**uiero** k) V**ale** l) No pasa **nada** m) Vamos a que**dar** n) ¿A qué **hora**?

10a. Complete with the suitable option
hola ; gracias ; qué ; dar ; apetece ; vale ; hora ; quedar ; bien ; del ; luego ; hasta

THE LANGUAGE GYM

10b. Complete with the suitable option

hola ; muy ; vamos ; ir ; me ; quiero ; nada ; fiesta ; a ; quedamos ; autobús ; luego

11. Faulty translation

a) **How** are you?   b) See you **later**.   c) **At what time** do we meet?   d) See you **later**.

e) It's ~~not~~ OK.   f) There is **no** problem.   g) We **can** go.   h) Very **well**.

i) I **don't** want to.   j) What do you want to do **today**?   k) I want to go **for a walk in the** centre.

l) I have to **do the chores**.

12. Find in the text the Spanish equivalent

a) ¿qué tal?   b) ¿Qué quieres hacer esta tarde?   c) ¿A qué hora quedamos?   d) nos vemos luego

e) ¿Dónde quedamos?   f) Vale, guay   g) me gustaría mirar escaparates   h) al lado del colegio

i) claro que sí   j) lo siento   k) a la casa de Amparo   l) tengo que ayudar a mi madre con las tareas

13. Answer in English

a) A little bit tired   b) She would like to go window shopping   c) Susana wants to go to Amparo's house

d) At six   e) Because she has to help her mother with the chores   f) In the café next to the school

14. Spot and correct the mistakes

a) ¿**A** qué hora quedamos?   b) Tengo **que** ayudar **a** mi madre   c) Vale. No pasa nad**a**   d) No **me** apetece   e) Hasta **luego**

f) ¿**D**ónde quedamos?   g) ¿Qué quieres est**a** tarde?   h) ¿A las siete **y** media?

15. Find the Spanish equivalent in the conversation above

a) estoy un poco aburrida   b) nada especial   c) arreglé mi habitación   d) corté el césped   e) me gustaría ir de tiendas

f) No sé, cariño   g) No pasa nada   h) La última película   i) tengo que lavar y planchar   j) delante de tu casa   k) genial

16. Answer in English

a) Fine   b) She did her homework, tidied her room and walked the dog

c) He went jogging, mowed the lawn and rode the bike   d) She wants to go shopping   e) He'd rather go to the cinema

f) She has to help her brother with his homework   g) She has to do the laundry and iron the clothes   h) 6.30

i) In front of Juan's house

17. Complete the table

Lo siento – **I am sorry**   **Estoy bien** – I am fine   **Genial** – Great   No puedo – **I can't**   No me apetece – **I don't fancy it**

Esta tarde – **This afternoon/evening**   **Delante de tu casa** – In front of your house   **¿A qué hora?** – At what time?

¿Dónde quedamos? – **Where shall we meet?**   ¿A qué hora quedamos? – **At what time shall we meet?**

No pasa nada – **Not a problem**

18. Complete with a suitable word

a) ¿Qué quieres **hacer**?   b) ¿Dónde **quedamos**?   c) A las cinco y **media**   d) Vamos a **quedar** enfrente de tu casa

e) ¿Qué **tal**?   f) Estoy un poco **aburrida**   g) No, no me **apetece**   h) Quiero ir al **cine** contigo

i) Tengo que ayudar a **mi padre** en la cocina   j) Tengo que **pasear** al perro

19. Complete

a) ¿**D**ónde **quedamos esta** tarde?   b) ¿**Qué q**uieres **hacer**?   c) **V**ale) **No pasa nada**   d) **Tengo que ayudar** a mis **padres**

e) **Lo siento**) No me **apetece**   f) **Quedamos e**nfrente **del cine**   g) **Tengo que arreglar** mi **habitación**

h) **Podemos ir al parque con ellas**   i) ¿**A qué hora quedamos**?   j) **Nos vemos luego**

20. Translate into Spanish

a) No pasa nada   b) ¿Quieres ir de tiendas?   c) No me gusta   d) No puedo porque tengo que estudiar

e) ¿Qué quieres hacer?   f) Tengo que ayudar a mi madre   g) Tengo que planchar la ropa   h) ¿Dónde quedamos?

i) Quedamos en la parada de autobús cerca de mi casa   j) ¿A qué hora quedamos?   k) Me gustaría ir a nadar/hacer natación

l) Lo siento, tengo que hacer mis deberes

21. Answer each of the questions below with a full sentence, as in the example

Accept any suitable answers.

22. Write the questions for the answers below

a) ¿Qué quieres hacer hoy?   b) ¿Por qué no?   c) ¿Qué hiciste ayer?   d) ¿Dónde quedamos?   e) ¿Te apetece ir al cine?

f) ¿Quieres ir al cine?   g) ¿Puedes quedar el viernes? / ¿Quedamos el viernes?

23. Translate 1 and 2 into English and 3 into Spanish

1.

M. Hi Julio. How are you?

J. All good, Marina. And you?

M. Fine, but I'm very tired.

J. Why?

M. Yesterday afternoon/evening I went jogging and then swimming. Also, I got up very early today.

J. Oh. Then you can't go out this evening?

M. Yes, of course I can! Where do you want to go?

J. To Fernando's party?

M. Yes, OK, cool. I fancy it. Where shall we meet?

J. Shall we meet at my house at seven?

M. Great. See you later.

2.

M. Hi Enrique. How are you?

E. Very well, Marcelo. And you?

M. What did you do last Saturday?

E. I went to buy groceries with my mother. And you?

M. I helped my father in the garden. It was boring!

E. Do you want to come with me to the stadium today?

M. Yes. That's cool! Where shall we meet, and at what time?

E. Let's meet in the bus stop opposite my house, at three.

M. OK, perfect. See you there at three.

3.

A. Hola Ana. ¿Quieres salir esta tarde?

C. Sí, pero primero tengo que ayudar a mi madre hasta las cuatro.

A. Vale. ¿Quieres ir al cine esta tarde?

C. No. Lo siento, pero no me apetece. Me gustaría ir al centro y mirar escaparates.

A. OK, no pasa nada. ¿A qué hora quedamos? ¿A las cuatro y medio?

C. No puedo a las cuatro y media. Tengo que ayudar a mi hermano con sus deberes. Vamos a quedar a las cinco.

A. Vale. A las cinco. ¿Dónde quedamos?

C. Vamos a quedar en tu casa.

Question Skills Unit 9

1. Match questions and answers

¿Qué haces para ayudar en casa? – Pongo la mesa y ayudo a mis padres

¿Qué hiciste ayer para ayudar a tu padre? – Pasé la aspiradora y preparé la cena

¿Qué te apetece hacer esta tarde? – Me apetece dar un paseo

¿Dónde quedamos? – Vamos a quedar enfrente de mi casa

¿A qué hora quedamos? – A las cinco

¿Por qué no puedes salir esta tarde? – Porque tengo muchos deberes y no tengo tiempo

¿Con quién vamos a ir? – Vamos a ir con Paco y Rafa

¿Adónde vais a ir? – No vamos a ir a ningún lado

¿Quieres jugar al tenis después? – Sí, es mi deporte favorito. Me encanta Nadal

2. Write the questions to the answers below

a) ¿Quieres ir al cine conmigo?   b) ¿A qué hora quedamos?   c) ¿Dónde quedamos?   d) ¿Con quién vais a ir?

e) ¿Qué haces para ayudar en casa?   f) ¿Qué hiciste ayer?   g) ¿Quieres quedar con tus amigos?

h) ¿Qué vais a hacer este fin de semana?

3. Break the flow

a) ¿Qué tal estás hoy?   b) ¿Qué quieres hacer hoy?   c) ¿Quieres ir al centro conmigo?   d) Sí me apetece mucho

e) ¿Dónde vamos a quedar?   f) ¿Con quién vamos a ir?

4. Spot and add in the one word missing from each sentence

a) ¿Qué haces para ayudar **en** casa?   b) ¿Qué **te** apetece hacer esta tarde?   c) ¿A qué **hora** quedamos?

d) ¿Te apetece ir **al** cine?   e) ¿Por **qué** no puedes salir después?   f) ¿Adónde vas **a** ir este fin de semana?

5. Fill in the gaps with appropriate questions

a) ¿Cómo estás?   b) ¿Y tú?   c) ¿Qué te gustaría hacer hoy?   d) ¿Te apetece?   e) ¿Dónde quedamos?

f) ¿A qué hora quedamos?   g) ¿Con quién vamos a ir?

Unit 10: Describing a typical day in the present, preterite & near future

1. Match: time markers

Ayer – Yesterday   **El sábado próximo** – Next Saturday   **Mañana** – Tomorrow   **El sábado pasado** – Last Saturday
Dentro de dos días – Within two days   **La semana pasada** – Last week   **El fin de semana** – At the weekend
Anteayer – The day before yesterday   **Hace unos días** – A few days ago   **El fin de semana pasado** – Last weekend

2. Complete the table

Hago – **I do**   Voy – **I go**   **Tengo que** – I have to   **Quiero** – I want   Salgo – **I go out**   Me levanto – **I get up**
Veo – **I see**   **Leo** – I read   **Escribo** – I write

3. Match: activities

Voy a levantarme temprano – I am going to get up early

Voy a leer un libro – I am going to read a book

Voy a estudiar – I am going to study

Voy a salir – I am going to go out

Voy a divertirme – I am going to have fun

Voy a ir de compras – I am going to go shopping

Voy a ayudar a mi hermano – I am going to help my brother

Voy a hacer deporte – I am going to do sport

Voy a montar en bici – I am going to ride a bike

4. Choose the correct translations

fui ; hice ; ayudé ; comí ; jugué ; quise ; bebí ; leí ; vi ; monté ; nadé

5. Break the flow

a) Ayer fui al cine con mi novia

b) Mañana voy a ir de compras con mi padre

c) La semana pasada fui de pesca con mi madre

d) Mi novia y yo vimos una película emocionante

e) Ayer no hice nada) Me relajé escuchando música

f) Por la tarde suelo ayudar a mi hermano con las tareas

g) Anteayer estudié mucho para la prueba de español

h) Esta tarde voy a montar en bici con mis amigos

i) El fin de semana hago mucho deporte

j) El fin de semana pasado hice pesas con mi primo

6. Complete the table with the options provided below

Ayer	Hoy	Mañana
Monté en bici	**Monto en bici**	Voy a montar en bici
Me levanté	Me levanto	**Voy a levantarme**
Salí con mi novia	**Salgo con mi novia**	Voy a salir con mi novia
Tomé un café	Tomo un café	**Voy a tomar un café**
Hice boxeo	**Hago boxeo**	Voy a hacer boxeo
Fui al cine	Voy al cine	**Voy a ir al cine**
Toqué la guitarra	**Toco la guitarra**	Voy a tocar la guitarra
Comí mucho	Como mucho	**Voy a comer mucho**

7. Translate into English

a) I went shopping   b) I am going to play chess   c) I read some comics   d) I ate seafood   e) I make my bed

f) I saw a film   g) I am going to get up   h) I played chess   i) I help my parents   j) I relaxed

 THE LANGUAGE GYM

k) I have to study   l) I usually go to bed late   m) I want to go out with my girlfriend

n) Today I cannot play   o) I have a lot of fun

8. Sentence puzzle

a) Ayer no hice nada especial   b) Anteayer vi una película   c) El fin de semana suelo hacer las tareas

d) El sábado pasado salí con mi novia   e) Todos los días tengo que levantarme temprano

f) Hace dos días jugué al ajedrez con mi padre   g) Esta tarde voy a ir a la playa   h) Ayer me relajé escuchando música

i) Mañana voy a montar en bici en el parque

9. Find in the wordsearch

a) jugué   b) voy a ir   c) veo   d) voy a levantarme   e) comí

f) fui   g) juego   h) hice   i) voy   j) hago

k) me relajé   l) monto   m) ayudo

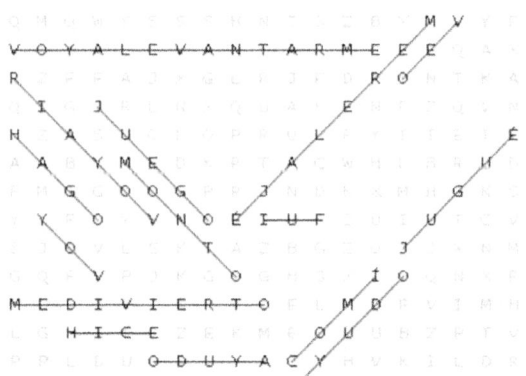

10. Complete with the correct option

a) ayudo   b) lavé, jugué   c) levantarme, voy a hacer

d) fui, vimos   e) suelo   f) tengo, odio   g) miré, fue

h) puedo, debo   i) hice, me relajé, leyendo   j) hago

11. Guided translation

a) **Jugué**   g) **Suelo comer**

b) **Voy a ir**   h) No **puedo**

c) **Veo**   i) **Fui**

d) **Hice**   j) **Voy a hacer**

e) **Tengo que**   k) **Ayudé**

f) No **quiero**   l) **Arreglé**

12. Complete with the correct verb in the appropriate tense

a) fui   b) leí   c) voy a ir   d) tengo que estudiar   e) suelo   f) voy a   g) salí   h) fui   i) quiero   j) suelo

k) montar   l) compré

13. Answer the questions about the text

a) Raúl   b) Roberta   c) Fernando   d) Carmen   e) Paco   f) Raúl   g) Beatriz   h) Paco's girlfriend   i) Roberta

j) Silvia   k) Carmen   l) Marina   m) Ale   n) Roberta   o) Susana

14. Find in the text the Spanish equivalent

a) suelo hacer muchas cosas   b) corrimos hasta las ocho y media   c) mi mejor amigo

d) nos divertimos mucho   e) no gano nunca   f) me encanta correr   g) solo durante media hora

h) paso la tarde jugando   i) nada especial   j) voy a ir de excursión   k) voy a comprar   l) hicimos turismo

m) dimos una vuelta por el centro   n) había mucho que ver y hacer

15. Correct the statements

a) At the weekend Txosi **does many things**

b) On Saturdays he gets up **very early**

c) He always **loses** at racket sports

d) In the afternoon he goes **rock climbing** with his father and **younger** brother

e) On Sundays he does **less** running than on Saturdays

f) On Sunday **afternoons** he spends time **playing** on his computer

g) They usually have dinner at his grandparents, who are very **funny** and **friendly**

h) Next weekend he is going to **go sightseeing** in Barcelona / visit **the Sagrada Familia**

i) He is going to buy **(a lot of) clothes**

j) He went **sightseeing** in the centre of the city

k) Txosi and Aitor met two girls from Madrid **and are still in contact**

16. Correct the mistakes in the translation of the last two paragraphs of Txosi's text

Next **weekend** will be different because I am going to go on a trip to Barcelona with my **school**. We are going to visit the Sagrada Familia and other monuments and historic **places** of the city. There are **curious shops** in Barcelona, therefore I am going **to buy a lot of clothes.**

Last **year** we went to Madrid and **I had a great time.** We **went sightseeing** in the morning and in the afternoon we went for a walk around the **city centre.** My friend Aitor and I met two very **beautiful and funny** girls from **Madrid.** We are **still** in touch with them.

17. Find in the text the Spanish equivalent for the following sentences

a) Lo que me gusta de   b) Hago muchas cosas   c) Por el bosque cerca de mi casa   d) Nos caímos algunas veces

e) Nadie se hizo daño   f) No había mucha gente   g) Fue muy agotador   h) Sé que la comida basura es mala (para la salud)

i) (Accept: Fuimos) Fui con mi mejor amigo a mirar escaparates   j) Conocimos a un par de chicas muy simpáticas

k) Pasamos todo el día   l) (Yo) pasé mucho tiempo   m) Charlando con ella

18. Gapped sentences

a) time   b) sport   c) rode the bike, forest   d) fell, hurt   e) lifted weights   f) went rock climbing   g) exhausting

h) window shopping   i) walking with them   j) chatting   k) go out with her

19. Answer the questions below in Spanish

a) *Montaron en bici   b) Fue muy agotador / La sesión fue muy agotadora   c) Hay dos centros comerciales (grandes)

d) Javier es muy fuerte (está como un toro)   e) Dieron un paseo con las chicas / pasaron el día paseando

f) Iker va a ir al cine con Ainhoa

*Early edition question says 'parque' not 'bosque'

20. Complete with the correct option

El sábado pasado Roberto hizo muchas cosas. Primero, **montó** en bici por el bosque. **Fue** divertido. Luego, Roberto y sus amigos **fueron** al gimnasio cerca de su casa. Hicieron pesas. Después de hacer pesas **hicieron** escalada en el parque. El domingo pasado, Roberto **salió** con sus amigos. Primero, **dieron** una vuelta en el centro de la ciudad y luego **miraron** escaparates en un centro comercial. Paco **conoció** a dos chicas muy divertidas y Roberto y él **pasaron** todo el día paseando con ellas. Roberto **pasó** horas hablando con Ana. El fin de semana siguiente Roberto y Ana **salieron** juntos. **Vieron** una película en el cine y luego **comieron** en un restaurante. Después de comer, **pasearon** juntos en el parque del barrio. Se **divirtieron** mucho.

21. Complete the table using the preterite

1) Fue al cine   2) Fueron al cine   3) Vi una película   4) Vieron una película   5) Salí   6) Salió   7) Ayudó a su madre

8) Ayudaron a su madre   9) Jugué al fútbol   10) Jugaron al fútbol   11) No hizo nada   12) No hicieron nada

13) Leí un libro   14) Leyó un libro   15) Dio una vuelta   16) Dieron una vuelta   17) Miré escaparates

18) Miró escaparates   19) Conoció a un chico   20) Conocieron a un chico   21) No estudié   22) No estudiaron

22. Guided translation

a) **Ayer salí con mis amigos**   b) **Fue agotador pero divertido**   c) **Hace tres días fui a una fiesta**

d) **Ayer lavé el coche de mi madre**   e) **Suelo levantarme a las seis y media**   f) **Hoy tengo que ayudar en casa**

g) **El sábado pasado hice natación**   h) **Hoy tiene que estudiar inglés**   i) **Ayer toqué el ukelele**

23. Translate into Spanish

a) Ayer vi una película   b) Hace dos días no hice mis deberes   c) Esta mañana no arreglé mi habitación

d) El domingo pasado fui al parque con mis amigos   e) Tengo que hacer mi/la cama y lavar el coche

f) Mañana voy a montar en bici   g) La semana próxima voy a ir a Madrid   h) Esta tarde/noche no voy a hacer nada

24. Translate into Spanish

a) Hace dos días hicimos footing   b) La semana pasada mis amigos y yo jugamos al golf

c) El domingo pasado visité a mis abuelos   d) Cada día (or todos los días) debemos poner y quitar la mesa

e) Hoy no puedo salir con mi novia   f) La semana próxima vamos a ir de compras

g) Anteayer estudié mucho   h) Una vez a la semana tenemos que sacar la basura

25. Translate into Spanish

Normalmente, mi familia y yo hacemos muchas cosas el fin de semana. Sin embargo, el fin de semana pasado no hicimos mucho.

Yo me relajé leyendo un libro, hice mis deberes y miré/vi una película en la televisión. Mis padres hicieron footing, luego hicieron algunas tareas domésticas y jugaron a las cartas. Mi hermano mayor hizo sus deberes y entonces tocó la guitarra todo el día. Mi hermano menor pasó todo el día en su ordenador y jugando a la PlayStation.

Fue un fin de semana aburrido, pero me relajé mucho. El fin de semana próximo quiero quedar con mis amigos e ir al cine. Voy a tocar el ukelele con mi amigo Pedro. Pedro tiene quince años y es muy divertido. Él es mi mejor amigo.

26. Translate into Spanish

En mi familia todos tienen que ayudar en casa. Por ejemplo, mi madre tiene que cuidar el jardín. Mi padre cocina. Mi hermano y yo tenemos que hacer nuestras camas y arreglar nuestras habitaciones. Mi hermana cuida al perro.

Nos gusta ayudar a nuestros padres pero también hacemos otras cosas. Por ejemplo, el fin de semana pasado yo lavé el coche de mi padre y lo ayudé en el jardín. Mi hermano limpió el salón y lavó la ropa. Mi hermana cortó el césped y sacó al perro. Mis padres estuvieron muy felices.

27. Complete with a suitable word

Accept any suitable answers.

28. Complete the sentences below

Accept any suitable answers.

29. Answer the questions below in Spanish and in full sentences

Accept any suitable answers.

30. Write a text including the points below

Accept any suitable answers.

Question Skills Unit 10

1. Complete with the missing words
a) ¿ **Dónde** vives?

b) En tu barrio, ¿qué lugares **hay**?

c) ¿**Vives** en una casa o en un piso?

d) ¿**Qué** se puede hacer en tu barrio?

e) ¿Qué **haces** para ayudar en casa?

f) ¿**Quién** ayuda más, tu hermano o tú?

g) ¿Qué **hiciste** ayer para ayudar?

h) ¿**Cómo** vas al colegio?

i) ¿A qué **hora** te despiertas?

j) ¿Cómo **es** tu casa?

k) ¿Desde **cuándo** vives allí?

l) ¿Dónde te **gustaría** vivir en el futuro?

2. Match questions and answers

¿A qué hora te despiertas? – Entre semana, me despierto a las siete

¿Vives en una casa o en un piso? – Vivo en una casa en el centro de la ciudad

¿Cómo es tu casa? – Mi casa es pequeña pero muy acogedora

¿Te gusta tu casa? – ¡Sí, me encanta mi casa!

¿Desde cuándo vives allí? – Vivo allí desde que nací

¿Cómo vas al colegio? – Normalmente voy al colegio a caballo

En tu barrio, ¿qué sitios hay? – Hay un parque, un restaurante y un museo

¿Qué se puede hacer en tu ciudad? – Se puede ir al cine, se puede hacer deporte y mucho más

¿Qué haces para ayudar en casa? – Arreglo mi habitación y preparo la cena

¿Qué hace tu hermano para ayudar? – Mi hermano no hace nada, es muy perezoso

¿Quién ayuda más, tu hermano o tú? – Yo ayudo mucho más. Mi hermano es muy vago

¿Dónde te gustaría vivir en el futuro? – Me gustaría vivir en Australia cuando sea mayor

3. Faulty translation
a) What do you do to help **your parents** at home?   b) What can you see in your **city**?

c) Which is your favourite place in your **neighbourhood**?   d) What is your **house** like?   e) Why do you **like** your house?

f) How long **have you lived** there?   g) What did **you** do yesterday to help at home?

h) Who helps more, your **brother** or yourself?   i) What time do you **wake** up in the morning?

4. Translate into Spanish
a) ¿Dónde vives?   b) ¿Te gusta tu casa?   c) ¿Desde cuándo vives allí?   d) En tu barrio, ¿qué lugares hay?

e) ¿Qué se puede hacer en tu ciudad?   f) ¿Qué haces para ayudar en casa?   g) ¿Quién ayuda más, tu hermana o tú?

h) ¿Qué hiciste ayer para ayudar en casa?

Vocab Revision Workout 5

1. Match
Mucho que hacer – A lot to do   **En mi casa** – In my house   **En mi ciudad** – In my town

Edificios antiguos – Old buildings   **En el norte** – In the north   **La gente** – The people

Para los jóvenes – For young people   **Me dolía el/la...** – My ... hurt   **Áreas verdes** – Green spaces

En mi calle – In my street   **Muchas cosas** – Many things

2. Complete with suitable words
a) Vivo en una **ciudad** en el sur de **España**

b) Mi barrio está en las **afueras** de la ciudad

c) No me gusta mi barrio porque es **feo**

d) No **hay** muchas tiendas ni **áreas** verdes

e) Hay mucho **crimen** también, así que no es un **lugar** seguro

f) Anoche no hice mis deberes porque me dolía mucho **la cabeza**

g) En mi calle hay solo una **tienda**

h) Vivo en un edificio **sucio** y antiguo. No me **gusta**

THE LANGUAGE GYM

3. Translate into Spanish

Vivo en una ciudad en el sur de España. Mi barrio está en las afueras de la ciudad. Mi barrio es grande y bonito. Hay muchas áreas verdes e instalaciones deportivas. También hay un centro comercial enorme cerca de mi casa con muchas tiendas buenas. En mi calle hay un gimnasio, un supermercado pequeño, un restaurante chino y un bar. Cerca de mi casa hay un parque grande donde monto en bici, juego con mis amigos y paseo al perro. Lo mejor de mi barrio es que la gente es amable y educada. Lo peor es que no hay mucho que hacer para los jóvenes.

4. Sentence puzzle

a) Ayer fui al cine con mi novia para ver una película   b) Anteayer monté en bici en el parque con mis amigos

c) Afortunadamente, se puede hacer mucho deporte en mi barrio   d) Hace tres días fui de compras al centro comercial

e) En mi barrio hay muchas tiendas de ropa buenas   f) En mi barrio se puede hacer muchas cosas

g) Se puede hacer escalada y patinaje en el parque   h) La semana pasada fui al polideportivo para jugar al tenis

i) Ayer fui al estadio con mi hermano para ver un partido de fútbol

j) Mi hermano y yo fuimos a ver un espectáculo de flamenco

5. Complete with *hacer, jugar, ir, ver* or *visitar* as appropriate

a) Se puede **hacer** natación   b) Se puede **ver** partidos de fútbol   c) Se puede **ir** de compras   d) No se puede **ver** conciertos

e) Se puede **visitar** palacios históricos   f) Se puede **jugar** al golf   g) Se puede **ver** películas   h) Se puede **ir** de marcha

i) Se puede **hacer** footing en el parque

6. Spot and correct the spelling errors

a) Edimburgo está en Escocia   b) Cerca de mi casa hay una calle peatonal   c) En mi barrio hay un parque grande

d) Me gusta mi barrio porque es seguro   e) Mi barrio está limpio y bien cuidado   f) En mi barrio hay mucho tráfico

g) En mi barrio se puede hacer footing en el parque   h) Ayer jugué al tenis en el club cerca de mi casa

i) Anteayer hice natación en la piscina municipal

7. Faulty translation

a) In my street there **are** many **good** shops

b) The tennis club is **in front of** the **school**

c) There are no **sports** shops in my **street**

d) Is there **any library** over here?

e) The park is located **opposite** the **train** station

f) There's a supermarket **near** the sports centre

g) The restaurant is a ten minutes **car ride away**

h) **Next to** my house there is a **baker's**

8. Translate into English

a) I went to the swimming pool   b) I am going to go shopping   c) We went to the countryside   d) We did sport

e) We are going to ride the bike   f) I went swimming   g) I am going to go to the stadium   h) We played basketball

i) We went sightseeing   j) I read a novel   k) I saw cartoons

9. Translate into Spanish

a) Lo pasé muy bien con mi mejor amiga   b) Fui al cine con mi novia   c) Hicimos turismo en el casco antiguo

d) Voy a jugar al baloncesto mañana   e) No hice nada el sábado pasado

f) Fuimos de compras en el centro comercial cerca de mi casa   g) Vamos a ir a una fiesta   h) Hice natación y monté en la bici

i) No hice mis deberes porque me dolía la cabeza   j) No lavé el coche porque tenía que estudiar   k) No lavé los platos ayer

Unit 11: Talking about a past holiday – where we went & where we stayed

1. Match
El barco – The ship/boat   **El coche** – The car   **El viaje** – The journey   **El hotel barato** – The cheap hotel
El hotel de lujo – The luxury hotel   **La granja** – The farm   **La casa de mis abuelos** – My grandparents' house
El avión – The plane   **La cancha de tenis** – The tennis court   **La semana pasada** – Last week   **La gente** – The people

2. Complete with the missing letter
a) Fui a Francia   b) Fui a Alemania   c) Fui a Japón   d) Fui a España   e) Fui a Italia
f) Fui a una isla en el Caribe   g) Fui a Escocia   h) Fui a Irlanda

3. Break the flow
a) El año pasado fui a Alemania   b) Fui allí con mi familia   c) Viajamos en coche   d) El viaje fue largo y aburrido
e) Me alojé en un hotel de lujo cerca de la playa   f) El hotel era grande y moderno
g) Lo pasé bomba porque el hotel era genial   h) Además, había mucho que hacer

4. Complete with a suitable word
Accept any suitable answers.

5. Faulty translation
a) Two **weeks** ago I went to Spain   b) The **boat** journey was very **slow**   c) Last **week**   d) I had a **great** time
e) There were fantastic **beaches**   f) We stayed in a **youth hostel**   g) There were a lot **to do**
h) **There was a tennis court**   i) My room was very **spacious**

6. Sentence puzzle
a) El mes pasado fuimos a España   b) Fui allí con mi mejor amigo   c) Viajamos en tren y luego alquilamos un coche
d) El viaje fue largo pero muy divertido   e) Me alojé en un hotel barato cerca de la playa
g) Lo pasé bomba porque las playas eran magníficas e hizo buen tiempo todos los días

7. Complete with *ir* in the preterite
a) fui   b) fue   c) fueron   d) fuimos   e) fuiste   f) fue   g) fue   h) fueron   i) fuisteis   j) fuimos   k) fue

8. Verb anagrams
a) pasé   b) hizo   c) fuimos   d) alojamos   e) había   f) comieron   g) jugó   h) hicimos

9. Gapped translation
a) month   b) rented   c) good   d) cheap   e) far from   f) liked   g) young people   h) boat   i) great time   j) parents

10. Translate into English
a) We traveled by boat   b) We went to Greece   c) I didn't go anywhere   d) There were great beaches
e) My parents had a great time   f) We went sightseeing every day   g) We stayed in a youth hostel
h) There was a lot to do for young people   i) We had a lot of fun   j) We went on a trip almost every day
k) People were very nice   l) We saw a lot of great places

11. Wordsearch
a) fui allí   b) con mi familia
c) viajé en barco   d) el viaje fue lento
e) nos quedamos   f) en un hotel
g) descansamos   h) lo pasamos bomba
i) la gente era simpática   j) hizo buen tiempo

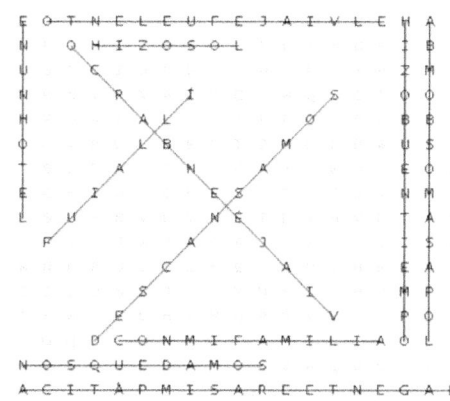

12. Categorise the sentences below with a T for "means of transport", an A for "accommodation" or a W for weather

a) A   b) T   c) A   d) W   e) T   f) T   g) W   h) A   i) T   j) A   k) A   l) W   m) A   n) W

13. Slalom writing

a) El viaje fue largo, aburrido y agotador   b) Nuestro hotel estaba cerca del centro

c) En el hotel había una sala de juegos para los niños   d) Mis padres fueron de compras

e) Mi hermana hizo turismo con su novio   f) Mi hermano y yo fuimos a la playa   g) Lo pasamos bomba. Quiero volver allí

14. Find in Orla's text the Spanish for

a) Alquilamos   j) Así que

b) El viaje   k) Buen tiempo

c) Bastante largo   l) Pudimos

d) Nos alojamos   m) Todos los días

e) Estaba muy cerca   n) Por las tardes

f) Había   o) Me quedé

g) Una sala de juegos   p) Pero

h) Una zona de spa   q) Mi hermano mayor

i) La comida   r) Fue de marcha

15. Answer the following questions about Aoife

a) Plane (and then car)   b) Short but quite boring   c) A cheap hotel (near Benidorm)   d) Not far / one km away

e) Very often   f) They went to local restaurants   g) Clothes and earrings   h) It had no water!

i) There were many nice young people

16. Find someone who…

a) Aoife   b) Ciara   c) Ciara   d) Ciara   e) Aoife   f) Orla   g) Aoife   h) Ciara   i) Orla   j) Ciara   k) Aoife

17. Complete with the options provided in the box below

El año pasado fui a **España**. Viajamos en **avión** y luego alquilamos un coche. El viaje fue bastante **largo** y aburrido. Nos alojamos en un hotel muy **barato** (pero bueno) en Málaga. El hotel estaba muy cerca del **centro** de la ciudad. Me gustó **muchísimo**. Había una piscina muy **grande**, una sala de juegos para los niños y una zona de spa para mis padres también. El restaurante servía comida muy **rica**, así que comimos mucho. Hizo **calor** todos los días, así que fuimos a la playa a menudo. Por las tardes no **salí**, pero mi hermano mayor fue de marcha todos los días.

18. Jigsaw reading

1, 9, 2, 4, 8, 5, 7, 3, 6, 10

19. Correct the following sentences from Aoife's text at page 141

a) El año pasado fui **a** España

b) El vuelo **fue** corto, pero bastante aburrido

c) Nos alojamos en un hotel barato cerca **de** Benidorm

d) El hotel estaba muy lejos del mar así que tuvimos **que** caminar mucho **para** ir a la playa

e) No **me** gustó mucho el hotel

f) El restaurante servía **comida** frita y grasienta ~~comida~~, así que no **comí** mucho

g) Afortunadamente, **hizo** buen tiempo casi todos los días

20) Complete the sentences below with any suitable word

Accept any grammatically correct & logical answers

21) Gapped translation

a) Clean **towels**

b) Well-**furnished**

c) There was no **soap**

d) It was **dirty**

e) There were **sea views**

f) Nothing **worked**

g) There were **cockroaches**

h) Old **furniture**

i) A dirty **pillow**

j) Clean **sheets**

k) It was **dirty**

l) A **new** TV

m) There was a **fridge**

n) A **comfortable** bed

22. Match

Limpia – Clean **Sucia** – Dirty **Funcionaba** – It worked **Nevera** – Fridge **Bien amueblada** – Well-furnished

Muebles – Furniture **Vistas al mar** – Sea views **Nueva** – New **Toallas** – Towels **Sábanas** – Sheets

Cucarachas – Cockroaches **Almohadas** – Pillows **Jabón** – Soap

23. Complete with the missing letters

a) Mi h**abitación** b) **Muebles** viejos c) Una cama c**ómoda** d) Nada f**uncionaba** e) **Almohadas** limpias

f) Había **cucarachas** g) Mal **amueblada** h) No había j**abón** i) S**ábanas** limpias j) Estaba s**ucio**

k) Estaba **limpia**

24. Match questions and answers

¿Adónde fuiste de vacaciones? – A Cancún, en México

¿Cuándo fuiste? – Fui el verano pasado

¿Cómo viajaste? – En avión, por supuesto

¿Con quién fuiste? – Con mi familia

¿Dónde te alojaste? – Nos alojamos en un hotel

¿Dónde estaba el hotel? – Estaba cerca de la playa

¿Cómo era el hotel? – Era un hotel de lujo, muy grande y moderno

¿Qué había en el hotel? – Una piscina muy grande, un gimnasio y tres restaurantes

¿Cuánto tiempo te quedaste allí? – Dos semanas

¿Cómo era tu habitación? – Muy limpia y acogedora

¿Qué había en tu habitación? – Había una cama grande, un escritorio y una tele

25. Complete with the missing letters

a) **Hace** dos años b) **Fuimos** a Alemania c) **Viajé** en avión d) Lo **pasamos** bomba e) **Fue** muy relajante

f) Me **quedé** en un campıng g) **Vi** muchos monumentos h) **Había** cucarachas i) **Casi** todos los días

j) La ducha no **funcionaba**

26. Translate into Spanish

a) El año pasado b) Viajé en coche c) Me quedé d) En un hotel barato e) Cerca de la playa f) Había

g) Una piscina grande h) Comida rica i) Hizo buen tiempo j) Casi todos los días k) Afortunadamente

l) Lo pasé bomba

27. Complete

a) **Fui** de v**acaciones** a E**spaña** b) **Viajé** en **coche** c) **Fui allí** con **mi familia** d) El **viaje** fue **largo**

e) **Nos** a**lojamos** en un **albergue juvenil** f) Me **gustó** mucho el **hotel** g) Lo pasé **bomba**

h) E**n el** h**otel** había **mucho que hacer** i) **Había** una **piscina**, u**n gimnasio y muchas otras cosas**

28a. Answer the questions as if you were Jorge

a) Fui a Italia b) Fui el año pasado c) Viajé/viajamos en avión d) Fui con mi mejor amigo, Leonardo

e) Me alojé/nos alojamos en un hotel (muy bueno) f) El hotel estaba en Sorrento

g) Era el hotel era moderno y cómodo (accept 'muy bueno')

h) Había una piscina, una sala de juegos (para niños) y una zona de spa

i) Me quedé una semana (accept alternative times) j) Era grande y cómoda (accept logical alternatives)

k) Había una cama grande y una televisión (accept logical alternatives)

l) La comida estaba buenísima m) Hizo buen tiempo todos los días

 **THE LANGUAGE GYM**

28b. Cast your mind back to a recent holiday of yours and answer the questions in 28a

Accept any suitable answers.

29. Translate into Spanish

a. El año pasado fui de vacaciones a España. Viajé en avión. Nos alojamos / Nos quedamos en un hotel de lujo en la costa de Andalucía. El hotel era muy bonito y moderno. Había muchas instalaciones deportivas. Además, había un pub y algunas tiendas de ropa muy agradables.

b. Afortunadamente hizo buen tiempo, por tanto, pudimos ir a la playa todos los días. La playa estaba solo a cien metros a pie del hotel. Todos los días tomamos el sol, nadamos, jugamos al vóleibol y paseamos por la orilla. Nos encantó la playa y allí la gente era muy agradable y simpática.

c. Me gustó mucho el hotel. Había muchas cosas para los jóvenes como yo, y también un área de spa para mis padres. La piscina y el gimnasio eran fenomenales. Por la tarde había conciertos en vivo y otros espectáculos. Mi habitación era grande y estaba bien amueblada. Había una televisión grande y un balcón grande con vistas al mar. Todo funcionaba perfectamente.

d. Mi amigo Paco también fue de vacaciones a España, pero él se quedó en Lloret de Mar, cerca de Barcelona en la Costa Brava. Fue allí con su madre y su hermana. Dijo que no hizo buen tiempo, por tanto no pudo ir a la playa todos los días. Le encanta la playa, así que estuvo muy decepcionado. Afortunadamente, había muchas tiendas buenas, así que compró muchas cosas para sí mismo y para su novia.

Question Skills Unit 11

1. Complete

a) fuiste   b) viajaste, cómo   c) quién   d) dónde, gustó   e) hiciste   f) probaste   g) qué   h) tuviste

2. Write a question for each of the answers

a) ¿Adónde fuiste de vacaciones?   b) ¿Cómo viajaste?   c) ¿Con quién fuiste?   d) ¿Dónde te quedaste?

e) ¿Te gustó el hotel? ¿Por qué?   f) ¿Qué tiempo hizo?   g) ¿Qué hiciste durante las vacaciones?

h) ¿Qué fue lo mejor de las vacaciones?   i) ¿Tuviste algún problema en el hotel?   j) ¿Te gustaría volver el año que viene?

3. Rewrite the questions in correct Spanish

a) ¿Adónde fuiste el año pasado?   b) ¿Cómo viajaste?   c) ¿Cómo fue el viaje? ¿Te gustó?   d) ¿Dónde te alojaste?

e) ¿Qué tiempo hizo?   f) ¿Qué hiciste durante el viaje?   g) ¿Te gustaría volver el año que viene?

4. Translate into Spanish

a) ¿Adónde fuiste el año pasado?   b) ¿Con quién fuiste?   c) ¿Cómo es él/ella?   d) ¿Cómo viajaste?   e) ¿Dónde te alojaste?

f) ¿Cómo era el hotel?   g) ¿Tuviste algún problema en el hotel?   h) ¿Qué hiciste durante las vacaciones?

i) ¿Probaste algún plato típico?   j) ¿Qué fue lo mejor de las vacaciones?   k) ¿Te gustaría volver el año que viene?

Unit 12: Talking about a past holiday – what we did and our opinion of it

1. Match

Alquilé una bici – I rented a bike   **Probé platos típicos** – I tried typical dishes   **Fui de marcha** – I went clubbing

Hice senderismo – I went hiking   **Compré recuerdos** – I bought souvenirs   **Tomé el sol** – I sunbathed

Hice buceo – I went scuba diving   **Descansé** – I rested   **Di un paseo** – I went for a walk

Conocí a un chico – I met a boy   **Fui de excursión** – I went on a trip   **Me acosté tarde** – I went to bed late

2. Missing letters

a) Alquilé una bici   b) Compré recuerdos   c) Tomé el sol   d) Hice buceo   e) Conocí a un chico simpático   f) Di un paseo

g) Probé platos típicos   h) Nadé en el mar   i) Hice senderismo   j) Saqué muchas fotos   k) Me acosté tarde

l) Fui de marcha

3. Faulty translation

a) On the **first** day   b) I went **hiking**   c) I went for a **walk**   d) I **rested**   e) I met a **boy**   f) I **tried** typical dishes

g) I did **hardly anything**   h) The **worst** thing was   i) I went **diving**   j) I swam in the **sea**   k) I rented a **bike**

l) I went to bed **late**

4. Spot and add the missing word

a) Por **la** tarde   b) Conocí **a** un chico   c) Tomé **el** sol   d) Alquilé **una** bici   e) Fui **de** excursión   f) Di **un** paseo

g) Jugué con **mis** primos   h) Nadé en **el** mar   i) No hice **casi** nada   j) Fui **de** marcha   k) **Me** gustaría volver

5. Sentence puzzle

a) El primer día no hice casi nada   b) Por la mañana fui a la piscina   c) Tomé el sol escuchando música

d) Mis padres se levantaron muy tarde   e) Mi hermano pequeño pasó todo el tiempo jugando en su móvil

f) A eso de las doce y media almorzamos en el restaurante del hotel

g) Después de la siesta fui a la playa cerca del hotel, pero no había nadie allí

6. Wordsearch

a) hice buceo

b) hice senderismo

c) me acosté tarde

d) tomé el sol

e) fui a la playa

f) viajé en barco

g) el viaje fue lento

h) nadé en el mar

i) descansé

j) leí tebeos

k) saqué fotos

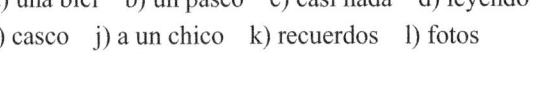

7. Gapped translation

a) On the **first** day, I did hardly **anything**   b) On the **second** day I went **hiking**   c) I **went** for a **walk** on the **beach**

d) I **relaxed** reading **comics**   e) I **met** a lot of nice **people**   f) One **day** we tried typical **dishes**

g) On the fourth day we went **sightseeing**   h) The **worst** thing was the **weather**   i) I **swam** and went **diving** every day

j) One day I **met** a Swedish **boy**   k) He was very **handsome** and **funny**

8. Complete with the correct option

a) una bici   b) un paseo   c) casi nada   d) leyendo   e) en el mar   f) tiempo   g) primer día   h) platos típicos

i) casco   j) a un chico   k) recuerdos   l) fotos

9. Complete the table

Español	English
Hice senderismo	**I went hiking**
Me desperté tarde	**I woke up late**
Saqué fotos	I took photos
Probé platos típicos	I tried typical dishes
El tercer día	**(On) the third day**
Pasé tiempo	**I spent time**
Tomé el sol	**I sunbathed**
Lugares históricos	Historic places
Fui de marcha	I went clubbing

10. Find someone who...

a) Roberta   b) Carlos   c) Felipe   d) Pablo   e) Marta   f) Verónica   g) Eugenia   h) Gabriel

11. Find the Spanish equivalent

a) Lo mejor fue cuando
b) Una motocicleta
c) Ropa bonita
d) Fuimos de tiendas
e) Cerca de mi hotel
f) Probamos
g) Un espectáculo de flamenco
h) Compré

i) Fuimos de excursión
j) Fue muy divertido
k) En la playa
l) Tan rica
m) Conocimos (a)
n) Una ciudad histórica
o) Incluso un castillo
p) Alquilamos

12. Translate into English

a) On the first day I didn't do much   b) I spent a lot of time with my family   c) I tried typical dishes
d) We went for a walk in the old city   e) We visited historic places   f) We saw dance shows   g) I went to bed late
h) I got up early   i) On the last day I saw a football match   j) I sunbathed on the beach

13. Anagrams

a) alquilé   b) dimos   c) fue   d) tomó   e) vimos   f) hice   g) probé   h) acosté   i) hicieron

14. Insert _yo, tú, él/ella, nosotros/as, vosotros/as_ or _ellos/as_ as appropriate

a) tú   b) ella   c) ellas   d) ellas   e) ella   f) nosotras   g) yo   h) ella   i) ellas   j) ellas

15 Complete the table

Alquilé	Alquiló	Alquilaron
Pasé	**Pasó**	**Pasaron**
Tomé el sol	Tomó el sol	Tomaron el sol
Conocí	Conoció	**Conocieron**
Hice	Hizo	Hicieron
Fui	Fue	Fueron
Di	Dio	**Dieron**
Vi	**Vio**	Vieron

16. Complete with the correct verb

a) El primer día f**uimos** de excursión   b) Mis padres h**icieron** senderismo cada día
c) Mi hermano j**ugó** al fútbol con sus amigos   d) **Pasamos** tiempo con nuestros abuelos   e) Me d**esperté** tarde todos los días
f) **Visitamos** lugares históricos   g) El último día f**ue** el mejor   h) **Dimos** una vuelta por el centro
i) Mi padre a**lquiló** un barco pequeño   j) S**aqué** muchas fotos de monumentos antiguos

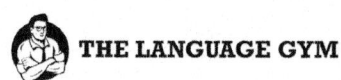

17. Rock-climbing translation

a) Un día alquilamos una bici y dimos una vuelta por el pueblo   b) Por la tarde me relajé escuchando música y leyendo

c) Fueron unas vacaciones inolvidables y me encantaría volver   d) Lo mejor fue cuando fuimos de marcha

e) El día antes de volver conocimos a dos chicas de Madrid

18. Guided translation

a) **Por la mañana fui** a la playa   b) No **hice casi nada**   c) **Pasé mucho tiempo con mis padres**

d) **Fueron unas vacaciones inolvidables**   e) **Mi hermano conoció** a una chica   f) **Mis padres hicieron senderismo**

g) **Nadé en la piscina. Me gustó**   h) **Me relajé leyendo en la playa**   i) **Nadamos en el mar**

19. Answer in English

a) By train   b) Near   c) On the beach/seashore   d) The weather was good every day

e) On the beach, sunbathing & doing water sports   f) They rested in the hotel   g) The day before returning (to Ecuador)

h) The Alhambra   i) Germany   j) Because they went to bed late

20. Tick the items that you can find (in Spanish) in Marcelo's text

a) √   f) √

b) √   g) √

c) √   h) √

d) √   i) X

e) √   j) X

21. Ross' text: find the Spanish equivalent

a) El invierno pasado   g) Fuimos de tiendas

b) Nos alojamos   h) Muchos recuerdos

c) Me gustó mucho   i) Ropa bonita

d) Había   j) Dos días antes

e) Mucha gente   k) Platos típicos

f) Descansamos   l) Conocimos

22. Ross' text: find the Spanish equivalent

a) invierno   b) coche   c) magníficas   d) descansamos   e) charlando   f) interesantes   g) recuerdos   h) pasamos

23. Jigsaw reading

1, 4, 9, 7, 10, 2, 11, 5, 12, 8, 6, 3

24. Complete with a suitable word

a) España, Valencia...   b) largo, agotador...   c) alojamos   d) mar   e) tiempo   f) fuimos

g) tomé, música   h) leí   i) vuelta   j) hacer   k) tiendas, muchas cosas   l) quedamos, televisión

25. Tangled translation: rewrite in Spanish

a) Un **día** hicimos **una** excursión a la **montaña**   b) Nos **quedamos en** un hotel cerca de la **playa**

c) En el hotel **había** muchas cosas que **hacer** para los **jóvenes**   d) Comimos **comida** muy **rica**

e) Afortunadamente hizo **buen tiempo** todos los **días**   f) Fuimos **a la playa** a menudo

g) Tomamos **el sol** y **jugamos** al voleibol   h) **Conocimos** gente simpática. Había muchos **chicos** guapos

i) Por la tarde **fui de compras**. Compré **muchas cosas**

26. Translate into Spanish

a) Hice senderismo   b) **Alquilé una bici**   c) **Pasé mucho tiempo**   d) **Jugué al tenis**   e) **Se levantó tarde**

f) **Hicimos turismo**   g) **Fuimos de compras**   h) **Nadamos en el mar**   i) **Fuimos de marcha**   j) **No hicieron nada**

27. Translate into Spanish

a) El primer día visité el casco antiguo   b) El segundo día alquilé una bici   c) El tercer día hicimos turismo

d) Por la mañana me levanté tarde   e) Tomé el sol en la playa hasta mediodía   f) Hicimos senderismo todos los días

g) Ayer di un paseo   h) Nadamos en el mar   i) Nos alojamos en un hotel barato

j) Por la noche mis padres fueron de marcha   k) Probamos platos típicos   l) Hizo buen tiempo todos los días

28. Complete the following sentences creatively

Accept any suitable answers.

29. Translate the paragraphs into Spanish

1. La semana pasada volví de Italia. Pasé una semana en Roma con mi familia. Me alojé en un hotel barato cerca de la estación de tren. Mi habitación era pequeña pero agradable. Visité el centro de la ciudad, muchos museos, ruinas romanas y vi muchos monumentos, iglesias y palacios antiguos. Lo mejor fue cuando conocí a un chico simpático de Argentina. Lo pasamos bomba juntos. También fui a la playa. La playa estaba a una hora de Roma en coche.

2. Hace dos meses mi hermano mayor fue a España solo. Se quedó en un pequeño pueblo de pescadores en la Costa Brava, a una hora de Barcelona. Alquiló una casa en la orilla. La casa estaba limpia y era agradable, pero no había televisión ni internet. La playa era genial, así que pasó todos los días tomando el sol, nadando y dando largos paseos por la orilla. Por las tardes probó platos típicos y después fue de marcha en Lloret de Mar.

3. El invierno pasado mis padres fueron a Francia. Pasaron dos semanas en Chamonix en los Alpes franceses. Se alojaron en un hotel de cuatro estrellas muy cerca de una fantástica pista de esquí. Las vistas eran magníficas. Nevó todos los días, así que hubo/había mucha nieve. Se levantaban temprano y esquiaban cada mañana y tarde durante una hora. No había mucha gente, así que fue muy divertido. Por la tarde comieron comida francesa. Estaba rica.

Question Skills Unit 12

1. Match questions and answers

¿Adónde fuiste de vacaciones? – Fui a Casares, cerca de Málaga

¿Cómo viajaste? – Viajé en avión porque es muy rápido

¿Cómo fue el viaje? – El viaje fue corto y relajante

¿Dónde te quedaste? – Me quedé en un camping

¿Cuántos días pasaste allí? – Pasé una semana y media allí

¿Qué hiciste el primer día por la mañana? – Me levanté temprano y desayuné una tostada

¿Qué hiciste por la tarde? – Después de comer, por la tarde, fui a la playa

¿Te gustaron las vacaciones? – Sí, mucho, fueron unas vacaciones geniales

¿Qué fue lo mejor de las vacaciones? – Lo mejor fue cuando nadé en el mar

¿Cómo prefieres viajar? – Prefiero viajar en tren porque es cómodo

¿Con quién prefieres viajar? – Prefiero viajar con mis amigos

¿Te gustaría volver el año próximo? – Sí, me encantaría volver a Casares

2. Write in the missing word

a) ¿Adónde **fuiste** de vacaciones?   b) ¿Cómo viajaste y **cómo** fue el viaje?   c) ¿**Cómo** prefieres viajar?

d) ¿Dónde **te** quedaste?   e) ¿**Qué** hiciste por la mañana?   f) ¿Qué **tiempo** hizo por la tarde?

g) ¿**Cuántos** días pasaste allí?   h) ¿Qué **hiciste** por la tarde?   i) ¿Qué fue lo **mejor** de la vacaciones?

j) ¿Te **gustaron** las vacaciones?   k) ¿Te **gustaría** volver el año próximo?

3. Write the questions to the answers below

a) ¿Adónde fuiste de vacaciones (el año pasado)?   b) ¿Cómo viajaste (y ¿por qué?)   c) ¿Dónde te quedaste?

d) ¿Qué hiciste por la mañana?   e) ¿Qué tiempo hizo el primer día?   f) ¿Cuántos días pasaste allí?

g) ¿Te gustó el albergue?   h) ¿Qué fue lo mejor de las vacaciones?   i) ¿Te gustaría volver otra vez / en el futuro?

4. Translate the following questions into Spanish

a) ¿Adónde fuiste de vacaciones el año pasado?   b) ¿Cómo viajaste?   c) ¿Cómo prefieres viajar?

d) ¿Con quién viajaste?   e) ¿Dónde te quedaste?   f) ¿Cuántos días pasaste allí?   g) ¿Qué fue lo mejor?

h) ¿Te gustaría volver el año próximo?

Vocab Revision Workout 6

1. Faulty translation
a) I didn't **clear** the table   b) I didn't **do** anything   c) I didn't **vacuum**   d) I washed the **car**   e) I tidied my **bedroom**
f) I didn't wash the **dishes**   g) I didn't **lay** the table   h) I **made** the bed   i) I **walked** the dog

2. Complete with a suitable word
a) tenía   b) dolía   c) estaba   d) no   e) le   f) tenía   g) pude   h) ganas   i) el   j) me

3. Translate
a) I couldn't do my homework   b) I didn't help my father   c) I didn't feel like it   d) I was busy   e) I didn't lay the table
f) I didn't do anything   g) My arm hurt   h) My head hurt   i) I usually wash the car   j) I didn't walk the dog

4. Complete with a suitable word
Marcelo: **Hola** Pablo, ¿qué tal?
Pablo: Hola Marcelo. Bien, ¿**y tú**?
Marcelo: Estoy bien. ¿**Qué** quieres hacer hoy?
Pablo: Hoy me gustaría **dar** un paseo en bici. ¿Y tú?
Marcelo: No sé, no me **apetece**. Yo quiero ir al cine.
Pablo: **Vale**, pues no pasa nada. Podemos ir al cine.
Marcelo: Fantástico. ¿A qué **hora** quedamos?
Pablo: Vamos a **quedar** a las siete.
Marcelo: Muy bien, ¿**dónde** quedamos?
Pablo: Vamos a quedar enfrente **del** cine.

5. Complete with the missing letters
a) ¿Dónde?   b) No p**uedo**   c) **Tengo** que   d) Hasta l**uego**   e) Me g**ustaría**   f) No q**uiero**   g) V**ale**
h) No pasa n**ada**   i) Vamos a que**dar**

6. Acro-translation
a) Nos vemos luego   b) Enfrente del cine   c) Tengo que hacer las tareas

7. Complete
a) ¿**Dónde** quedamos **esta** tarde?   b) ¿Qué **quieres** hacer?   c) **Vale**. No pasa nada
d) No puedo. **Tengo** que a**yudar** a mis p**adres**   e) Lo **siento**. No me apetece   f) **Vamos** a quedar enfrente del cine
g) **Tengo** que a**rreglar** mi h**abitación**   h) **Podemos ir** al **parque con ellas**   i) ¿A qué **hora** quedamos?

8. Sentence puzzle
a) Ayer no hice nada especial   b) Anteayer vi una película   c) El fin de semana suelo hacer las tareas
d) El sábado pasado salí con mi novia   e) Todos los días tengo que levantarme temprano
f) Hace dos días jugué al ajedrez con mi padre   g) Esta tarde voy a ir a la playa
h) Ayer por la tarde me relajé escuchando música

9. Complete with the correct verb in the appropriate tense (preterite, present or future)
a) fui   b) leí   c) voy a ir   d) tengo que   e) hacer   f) voy a   g) salí   h) fui   i) quiero   j) suelo   k) levantarme

 **THE LANGUAGE GYM**

Unit 13: Talking about a recent day trip

1. Match

Ayer por la mañana - Yesterday morning

Con mis padres - With my parents

Me levanté tarde - I got up late

Tomé una tostada - I had a piece of toast

Viajé en coche - I travelled by car

Hizo buen tiempo - The weather was good

Fui al campo - I went to the countryside

Me desperté temprano - I woke up early

Desayuné en la cocina - I had breakfast in the kitchen

Salí de casa - I left the house

El viaje fue largo - The trip was long

2. Complete

a) **viaje** b) **desperté** c) **juntos/as** d) **sol** e) **campo** f) **orilla** g) **cené/comí** h) **genial** i) **buen** j) **bien** k) **lago**

3. Gapped translation

a) yesterday | beach b) parents | late | day c) the house d) pool e) plane f) long g) arrived/got to h) things
i) swam | girlfriend

4. Arrange in chronological order (accept other logical solutions)

1, 4, 8, 10, 6, 13, 3, 9, 11, 7, 12, 5, 2

5. Break the flow

a) Me desperté temprano   b) Me levanté y me duché enseguida   c) Luego desayuné con mi hermano

d) Mis padres desayunaron más tarde   e) Viajé en autocar y luego alquilé un coche   f) Hicimos un picnic en la orilla del mar

g) Afortunadamente hizo buen tiempo   h) Nadamos en el mar y tomamos el sol

6. Verb anagrams

a) desperté b) viajamos c) llegamos d) era e) hizo f) hice g) tomó h) caminaron i) jugó

7. Likely or unlikely?

a) Likely   b) Unlikely   c) Unlikely   d) Likely   e) Unlikely   f) Likely   g) Unlikely   h) Unlikely   i) Likely   j) Unlikely
k) Likely

8. Multiple choice quiz

I woke up (2)   In the morning (3)   Before going to bed (1)   We came back late (3)   We arrived early (2)
The journey was slow (1)   We wenk hiking (3)   We fished in the river (2)   The journey was long (3)   We rented a car (1)

9. Complete with the options in the box

a) temprano b) desayuné c) levantaron d) salimos e) campo f) había g) gente h) sol i) nadé j) jugó
k) hizo l) tomaron m) volvimos

10. Write Yo, Él/Ella, Nosotros or Ellos as appropriate (also accept nosotras/ellas)

a) yo b) nosotros c) él/ella d) nosotros e) nosotros f) ellos g) yo h) nosotros i) ellos j) él/ella

11. Categories

Yo 1, 7, 12   Mi hermano 4, 6, 10, 14   Nosotros 2, 5, 9   Mis padres 3, 11, 15   El tiempo 8, 13, 16

12. Sentence puzzle rewrite the sentences in the correct order

a) Ayer fuimos de excursión al mar   b) Nos levantamos muy temprano   c) Salimos del hotel a eso de la siete

d) El viaje fue largo y un poco aburrido   e) Llegamos a la playa a eso de las ocho y media

f) La playa era magnífica, pero había muchísima gente   g) Mis padres tomaron el sol

h) Yo nadé y luego jugué al voleibol con mis hermanos   i) A eso de las cuatro llovió así que tuvimos que volver al hotel

j) El viaje de vuelta fue muy aburrido

13. Translate into English

a) I got up early

b) We got to the lake at around nine

c) It was sunny until four, then it rained

d) We didn't do anything special

e) My brothers did many things

f) The water in the sea was clean

g) My parents went water skiing

h) I walked along the seashore) It was relaxing

i) We returned to the hotel before dinner time

j) Before going to bed I had a shower and watched TV

14. Tangled translation: rewrite in Spanish

a) Ayer **por la mañana** me desperté **a** las **seis**

b) Fui a la **piscina con** mi **mejor** amigo

c) Me desperté muy **temprano**

d) Tomé el **desayuno** con mi **familia**

e) **Salí** de **casa** a las **siete**

f) Viajamos en **coche** con mi **padre**

g) El viaje **fue** largo **pero divertido**

h) Hizo **buen tiempo** por la **mañana**

i) Llegamos a la **playa a** las diez

j) **La** playa **era** magnífica

k) **Hicimos** muchas **cosas** juntos

l) Yo tomé el **sol** escuchando **música**

m) Mi hermano **nadó** en el **mar**

n) Mis **padres** caminaron por **la orilla**

15. Collocation puzzle put each item where it fits best (you can only use each number once)

Alquilamos 15, 25   Comimos 11   Conocimos 2, 12, 22   Fuimos 17, 23   Hicimos 4, 5   Hizo 14, 18
Jugamos 10, 20   Nos levantamos 6, 19, 21   Leímos 13, 16   Tomamos (1) 7, 8   Viajamos 3, 9, 24

16. Spot and add in the missing words

a) **el**   b) **en**   c) **fue**   d) **Por**   e) **en**   f) **el**   g) **la**   h) **no**   i) **un**

17. Complete with a suitable word (accept other grammatically correct & logical answers)

a) temprano / tarde   b) una tostada   c) cereales   d) desayunó   e) nueve   f) coche / autocar   g) una hora / dos horas

h) diez   i) buen tiempo / sol   j) el mar   k) senderismo   l) tomaron   m) una ensalada   n) volver   o) cinco   p) acostamos

18. Translate the following sentences into Spanish

a) Me levanté temprano

b) Desayuné

c) Comí una tostada con mermelada

d) Salimos del hotel

e) Viajamos en coche

f) Llegamos a las nueve

g) El viaje fue largo

h) Hizo buen tiempo

i) Hizo calor

j) Nadamos en el mar

k) Hicimos buceo

l) Mi hermano tomó el sol

m) (Él) jugó al voleibol

n) Mis padres descansaron

o) (Ellos) leyeron un libro

p) Durmieron

19. Find the Spanish equivalent

a) Pasé un día   b) Una ciudad costera   c) Se puede comer   d) Marisco muy fresco   e) Nos despertamos

f) Tomé una tostada   g) Salimos de casa a las nueve   h) Viajamos en coche   i) Mi padre pone música

j) Se marea mucho   k) Una vez vomitó

20. Gapped translation

a) small | house | outskirts   b) cereals | milk | orange juice   c) travelling | car | music | like   d) walk | seashore | swam | sea

e) ate | prawns | chicken | salad

21. Answer the questions in English

a) Alicante / small but modern house in the outskirts   b) Nothing to eat & a coffee   c) His dad puts on music that he likes

d) He gets sick/carsick (and vomits sometimes!)   e) They went for a walk along the seashore and then swam in the sea

f) Very nice / good and not very cold   g) In a restaurant called El Pescador, near the marina   h) He slept for the whole trip

22. Correct the wrong statements (not all are wrong)

a) a **coastal** town   b) many **lovely** beaches and **excellent** restaurants   c) on **his brother Jaime** while in the car d) -

e) weather is **almost always** good   f) clean and **not very cold** (N.B. This is very similar so can also be accepted as correct)

g) the most important thing for Pablo is **to have a good time**   h) reading a book and **sunbathing   i) -**

j) Pablo listened to music and **watched television** before going to bed

23. Tick or cross? Tick the phrases below that are contained in the text above and the cross the ones that are not.

a) √   b) √   c) X d) √   e) √   f) X   g) √   h) X   i) √   j) X   k) √   l) √   m) X   n) X   o) √

24. Translate Part 4 of the text into English

It was sunny and hot all day. The weather is almost always good on the Costa Blanca (the coast of Alicante). When we got to the Torrelamata beach we took a walk along the seashore and then we swam in the sea. The water was very nice: clean and not very cold. Later, I played volleyball with my brother. I play a little better than him, but it is not important. The most important thing is to have fun. Then I read a book and relaxed in the sun.

25. Wordsearch: find the Spanish translation of the sentences below and write them as shown in the example

a) Me levanté temprano   b) Fuimos al campo   c) Desayuné

d) Nadamos en el lago   e) Un vaso de leche   f) Salimos de casa

g) Viajé en coche   h) Sacaron muchas fotos   i) El viaje fue largo

j) Descansaron

* Mis padres tomaron el sol (not in the Wordsearch – sorry! 😊)

26. Guided translation

a) **Hace dos días hice una excursión**

b) **Salimos de casa temprano**

c) **Viajamos en coche**

d) **El viaje fue largo y aburrido**

e) **Llegamos a la playa a las ocho**

f) **La playa era magnífica**

g) **Hizo buen tiempo**

h) **Mi madre hizo esquí acuático**

i) **Tomé el sol y leí un libro**

j) **Mi hermano jugó al voleibol**

k) **Lo pasamos bomba**

27. Complete with the correct option

a) excursión   b) despertó   c) vistió   d) desayuno   e) un café   f) tuvo   g) viajaron   h) duró   i) llegaron   j) lago   k) tomó   l) quiso   m) relajó   n) salvajes   o) insectos

28. Find the Spanish equivalent in Carolina's text

a) Me quedé en casa   b) Miguel se despertó muy temprano   c) Se duchó, se vistió   d) ...y tomó un café

e) Salió de casa   f) El viaje duró dos horas   g) Cuando llegó a la playa   h) Miguel dio un paseo por la orilla

i) Jugaron al *voleibol   j) Se bañaron muchas veces   k) Fueron a un chiringuito   l) Se relajaron charlando

m) **...es un crack tocando la guitarra   n) Volvieron a casa a las cuatro   o) La próxima vez iremos juntos

*or football (early edition)

** not Miguel himself (early edition)

29. Complete the table

Almorzaron ; Nadó en el mar ; Alquilé un coche ; Tomó el sol ; Tomaron el sol ; Caminé por la orilla ;

Caminaron por la orilla ; Jugué al voleibol ; Saqué fotos ; Sacó fotos ; Me levanté tarde ; Se levantaron tarde ;

Hicieron senderismo ; Fui al campo ; Fue al campo ; Volvió a las ocho ; Volvieron a las ocho

30. Write two texts in Spanish, one in the first person (*yo*) and one in third person (*él/ella*)

1. Hace dos días fui de excursión en el campo con mi familia. Me desperté muy temprano, a eso de las cinco. Me duché, me vestí y desayuné con mi hermano. Comí un plátano y bebí café con leche. Mis padres se levantaron más tarde. Salimos de casa a las siete y media. Viajé en coche y el viaje duro más o menos una hora. Llegué a la granja de mis tíos a las ocho y media. Mi hermano y yo fuimos al lago con mis primos, y mis padres hicieron senderismo con mis tíos. Hacía buen tiempo, así que nadé en el lago y luego tomé el sol. Más tarde mis padres vinieron al lago. Tomaron el sol leyendo y charlando con mi tío y tía. Hicimos un picnic en el lago. Después de comer hice senderismo solo y vi animales salvajes y saqué fotos de insectos y flores. Fue muy relajante.

2. Ayer mi amigo Miguel fue de excursión al mar. Se despertó muy temprano, a eso de las seis. Se duchó, se vistió y desayunó con su familia. Comió dos huevos y bebió café. Su hermano y hermana se levantaron más tarde, y salieron de casa a eso de las ocho y cuarto. Viajaron en autobús y el viaje duró unos cuarenta y cinco minutos. Llegaron a la playa a eso de las nueve. Miguel y sus hermanos jugaron al voleibol y sus padres fueron a pasear por la orilla. El tiempo era muy caluroso/cálido, así que, después de jugar al voleibol, todos se bañaron en el mar. Sus padres conocieron a gente agradable y charlaron con ellos. A mediodía comieron bocadillos y bebieron café. Luego/Entonces Miguel tomó el sol escuchando música y fue muy relajante. Fue un día genial. Todos lo pasaron bomba.

Question Skills Unit 13

1. Match questions and answers

¿Adónde fuiste? – Fui a Marbella

¿A qué hora te despertaste? – Muy temprano, a eso de las seis de la mañana

¿A qué hora te levantaste? – Me levanté a las seis y cuarto

¿Cómo viajaste? – En coche hasta la estación y luego en tren

¿Cómo fue el viaje? – Un poco aburrido pero cómodo

¿Qué hiciste por la mañana? – Desayuné y luego fui a la playa

¿Qué hiciste por la noche? – Cené con mi familia en un restaurante típico

¿Qué atracciones turísticas visitaste? – Un castillo medieval y una catedral

¿Cuántos días te quedaste allí? – Solo nos quedamos un día

¿A qué hora volviste a casa? – Volví a casa a las diez de la noche

¿Qué fue lo mejor del día? – Cuando fuimos a la playa. Fue muy divertido

¿Qué hiciste antes de acostarte? – Me duché y fui a la cama enseguida

2. Complete with a suitable question word

a) Cuándo   b) Qué   c) Qué   d) Cómo   e) Cuántos   f) Cómo   g) Quién   h) Cuánto   i) Cuándo

3. Translate into English

a) How did you go?   b) Where did you go?   c) Did you have fun?   d) Whom did you meet?   e) What did you see?

f) What was the best thing?   g) How much time did you spend sightseeing?   h) How was the weather like?

4. Sentence puzzle rewrite the sentences

a) ¿Qué hiciste antes de acostarte?   b) ¿Cómo viajaste?   c) ¿Cómo fue el viaje?

d) ¿Qué hiciste por la mañana?   e) ¿Adónde fuiste?   f) ¿A qué hora te despertaste?

g) ¿A qué hora volviste a casa?   h) ¿Qué fue lo mejor del día?

i) ¿Qué atracciones turísticas visitaste?   j) ¿Cuántos días te quedaste allí?

5. Spot and correct the mistakes

a) ¿Adónde fuiste?   b) ¿Qué hiciste antes de acostarte?   c) ¿Qué **atracciones** turísticas visitaste?

d) ¿**A** qué hora te despertaste?   e) ¿Cómo fu**e** el viaje?   f) ¿**Có**mo viajaste?   g) ¿A qu**é** hora **te** levantaste?

h) ¿Qué fue lo mejor **del** viaje?   i) ¿Qué hiciste **por** la tarde?   j) ¿Cuánto**s** días **te** quedaste allí?

6. Write a question for each of the answers below

a) ¿Adónde fuiste?   b) ¿Cómo viajaste?   c) ¿Qué visitaste?   d) ¿A qué hora te levantaste?   e) ¿Qué fue lo mejor?

f) ¿Cómo fue el viaje?   g) ¿Cuántos días te quedaste allí?   h) ¿Cuándo llegaste a casa?   i) ¿Cómo era la gente?

j) ¿Qué hicisteis allí?

Unit 14: Talking about when I went to *La Tomatina* festival

1. Match

Fui a Buñol – I went to Buñol

Ella se despertó – She woke up

El viaje fue duro – The trip was hard

Hay algunas reglas – There are some rules

Tirar piedras – To throw stones

Llevar ropa vieja – To wear old clothes

Para participar en – To take part in

Alquilamos un coche – We rented a car

Llegamos temprano – We arrived early

No se debe – One must not

Se recomienda – It's recommended

Estuvo nublado – It was cloudy

2. Missing letters

a) El fin de semana pasado b) Fui a Buñol c) Me desperté muy temprano d) El día del festival e) En esta fiesta

f) Hay algunas reglas importantes g) Solo se debe tirar tomates h) Por la mañana i) Durante la batalla de tomates

j) Me caí muchas veces k) Me ensucié mucho

3. Faulty translation

a) My **best** friend b) **He/she** woke up at eight c) We arrived **early** d) There are **important** rules e) To throw **bottles**

f) Swimming **goggles** g) It was **stormy** h) I got really **dirty** i) I **laughed** a lot j) I returned **to the hotel**

k) I **went to bed** at ten

4. Spot and add in the missing word

a) Viajé **en** coche b) El viaje **fue** largo c) El día **del** festival d) Llegamos **temprano** e) No **se** debe tirar

f) Por **la** mañana g) Llovió un **poco** h) Me caí **muchas** veces i) Volví **al** hotel j) Me acosté **a** las 10

k) Me ensucié **mucho**

5. Sentence puzzle

a) El fin de semana pasado fui a Buñol b) Para participar en la Tomatina c) Llegamos temprano para coger sitio

d) En esta fiesta hay algunas reglas importantes e) No se debe tirar piedras o botellas f) Por la tarde llovió un poco

g) Durante la batalla de tomates h) Conocí a mucha gente divertida i) Me reí mucho y me ensucié mucho

6. Complete with the verb in the preterite form

a) La semana pasada yo **fui** a Buñol b) Mi amigo y yo **viajamos** en tren

c) **Me levanté / Nos levantamos** temprano, a las ocho d) **Llegué / llegamos** temprano para coger sitio

e) **Conocí / conocimos** a mucha gente divertida f) Yo **volví** al hotel a pie g) Nosotros **tiramos** muchos tomates

h) **Me ensucié / nos ensuciamos** mucho i) Volví al hotel y **me duché** j) Luego **descansé**

k) Mi amigo y yo **nos acostamos** a las 10 l) **Fue** un viaje inolvidable

7. ¿Buena idea o mala idea?

a) Mala idea b) Buena idea c) Buena idea d) Mala idea e) Buena idea f) Mala idea g) Mala idea

8. Gapped translation

a) weekend b) take part c) best d) travelled e) some f) stones g) good h) rained i) fight j) dirty

9. Translate into English

a) In the morning b) It was cloudy c) But later the weather was good/nice d) I met a lot of people e) I fell many times

f) And I laughed a lot g) We threw a lot of tomatoes h) We returned to the hotel i) We showered

j) We went (out) to eat tapas k) I went to bed at 10 l) It was a wonderful experience

10. Sentence puzzle: rewrite the sentences in the correct order

a) Fui a Buñol para participar en la Tomatina b) Viajé en avión y luego alquilé un coche c) El viaje fue largo pero divertido

d) Durante la batalla de tomates hay algunas reglas e) No se debe tirar botellas f) Se debe llevar una camiseta vieja

g) Conocí a un chico muy simpático h) Me ensucié mucho pero me reí un montón

THE LANGUAGE GYM

64

11. Find someone who…

…thinks there are too many rules - **Rafi**

…got really dirty but had a great laugh - **Leonardo**

…went to Buñol a long time ago - **Rosa**

…experienced a storm in the afternoon - **Dylan**

…thinks the rules are important for safety - **Natasha**

…thought it was like a big tomato soup - **Sara**

…had really good weather all day - **Mateo**

…went for food straight after the tomato fight - **Vero**

…was happy once they were got clean - **Jaume**

…had an unforgettable experience - **Ariella**

…loves that they could meet new people - **Mateo**

…kept falling over and found it disgusting - **Sara**

12. Gapped translation

a) A week **ago** I **went** to Buñol with my **best** friend to take part in the Tomatina

b) We **travelled** by plane because it is **fast** and then we rented a **car**

c) The **journey/trip** was long and **hard**) I got really **bored** and my friend **too/also**

d) On the **day** of the festival we **arrived** early to **get** a good spot

e) It is **recommended** that you wear **trainers** and old **clothes**

f) One should not throw **stones** nor **bottles**, only **tomatoes**

g) I met lots of fun **people** and **I laughed** a lot) I also got really **dirty**

13a. Complete the grid with the appropriate preterite <u>reflexive</u> verb forms

me acosté – **nos acostamos**   me desperté – nos despertamos   me reí – **nos reímos**   me caí – nos caímos

13b. Complete the grid with the appropriate preterite <u>regular</u> verb forms

conocí – **conocimos**   descansé – descansamos   viajé – **viajamos**   volví – volvimos

14. Complete with a suitable word

Accept any correct suggestion.

15. Find the Spanish equivalent

a) Fue increíble   b) Participar en   c) Nos despertamos   d) Alquilamos un coche   e) Llegamos temprano   f) Durante la fiesta

g) Hay algunas reglas   h) Gafas de natación   i) Hizo buen tiempo   j) Tiramos   k) ¡Lo pasamos bomba!   l) Luego fuimos

m) Una experiencia inolvidable

16. Answer the questions in Spanish in full sentences, as if you were Juanjo

a) Fui el fin de semana pasado   b) Fui con mi mejor amigo, Cristobal   c) Viajé en avión (y luego alquilé un coche)

d) ¡Es muy importante solo tirar tomates!   e) Porque los tomates son (bastante) ácidos (y te pueden dañar los ojos)

f) Hizo buen tiempo por la mañana   g) Conocí a mucha gente divertida (y tiré muchísimos tomates)

h) Cuando volví al hotel me duché (y luego fui a un restaurante)   i) Sí, me encantaría volver otra vez

17. Complete the sentences

a) funny | sporty   b) woke up | five   c) listening | looking at   d) early | good spot   e) stones | bottles | dangerous

f) returned | showered

18. Find the Spanish equivalent

a) fue bastante interesante   b) para participar en   c) tocar el ukelele   d) el día del viaje   e) no fue nada divertido

f) para coger sitio   g) pero yo solo tenía sandalias   h) esto sí es obvio   i) llovió un poco   j) odio los tomates

k) no me gustaría volver nunca

19. Translate into English the following sentences from the text above

a) Near the city of Valencia   b) I woke up at five   c) In fact, it was very boring   d) There are many interesting rules

e) One should only throw tomatoes   f) But it was too hot   g) In the afternoon/evening I returned to the hotel

h) It was a terrible experience

20. True, False, or Not mentioned Write T/F/NM & correct the wrong statements

a) **T**   b) **F** – It was not fun at all   c) **F** – They arrived early   d) **F** – He only had sandals   e. **NM**

f) **F** – He didn't like the weather at all   g) **T**   h) **F** – He never wants to return

21. Complete the text below with one of the options below

El mes pasado, (1) **fui** con mi primo a Buñol, para participar en la Tomatina. El día del viaje me desperté muy temprano, a las seis. Luego viajé en avión y luego (2) **alquilé** un coche. El viaje fue largo pero muy divertido. Me lo pasé genial (3) **escuchando** música y hablando con mi primo. El día del festival llegamos muy temprano para coger (4) **sitio**. Durante la fiesta de la Tomatina hay (5) **algunas** reglas muy importantes. La más importante es que solo se (6) **debe** tirar tomates. Por la mañana (7) **llovió** mucho y hubo tormenta, pero luego por la tarde (8) **hizo** buen tiempo. Durante la (9) **batalla** de tomates conocí a mucha gente guay y mi primo y yo nos (10) **reímos** muchos. Por la tarde volví al hotel y me (11) **duché**. Luego fui a un restaurante local con mi (12) **primo** y comimos unas tapas deliciosas. (13) **Fue** una experiencia inolvidable. Me (14) **gustaría** volver otra vez el año que viene.

22. Jigsaw reading arrange the text in order

5, 9, 1, 6, 4, 2, 8, 10, 7, 3, 11

23. Translate the sentences below into Spanish using: *(no) se debe + infinitive*

a) Se debe llevar ropa vieja   b) Solo se debe tirar tomates   c) Se debe llevar gafas de natación   d) No se debe tirar botellas

e) No se debe tirar piedras   f) Se debe llevar zapatillas (de deporte)

24. Translate the sentences below into Spanish using the preterite tense

a) me desperté   b) fui   c) viajé   d) llegué   e) conocí   f) tiré   g) me caí   h) me reí   i) me ensucié mucho

j) volví   k) descansé   l) comí

25. Translate the sentences below into Spanish using the preterite

a) Nos despertamos muy temprano   b) Conocimos a mucha gente divertida   c) Nos reímos mucho

d) Nos ensuciamos mucho   e) Nos caímos muchas veces   f) Comimos tapas.

26. Guided translation

a) El verano pasado fui a Buñol   b) Fui con mi mejor amigo Juan   c) Fuimos para participar en la Tomatina

d) Hay algunas reglas importantes   e) Solo se debe tirar tomates   f) Por la mañana hizo sol, pero luego llovió

g) Durante la batalla tiré muchos tomates   h) Conocí a gente divertida y me ensucié mucho

27. Translate the following text into Spanish

Hola. Me llamo Pedro. El año pasado fui a España, a Buñol cerca de Valencia. Fui para participar en la Tomatina. Fui con mi mejor amigo Tomás. Él es amable y gracioso. Viajamos en avión y luego en tren. El viaje fue muy largo pero bastante divertido. El día del festival llegamos bastante temprano para coger sitio. En este festival hay algunas reglas importantes. No se debe tirar piedras, solo tomates. Además, se recomienda llevar gafas protectoras/de natación y zapatillas de deporte. Por la mañana, hizo buen tiempo y mucho calor. Luego/Más tarde, hubo una tormenta y llovió mucho. Durante la batalla de tomates tiré un montón de tomates, me reí mucho y me ensucié mucho. Por la tarde volvimos al hotel, nos duchamos y luego comimos unas tapas. Me acosté a las diez. Fue una experiencia inolvidable y me gustaría volver el año que viene.

28. Write a 150 to 250 words paragraph in which you talk about a make-believe trip to the Tomatina festival.

Students own answer, based on language from this unit.

Question Skills Unit 14

1. Match questions and answers

¿Adónde fuiste? – Fui a Buñol, cerca de la ciudad de Valencia.

¿Con quién fuiste? – Fui con mi primo.

¿Cómo viajaste? – Viajé en avión y luego alquilamos un coche.

¿Cómo fue el viaje? – Fue largo, pero el vuelo me gustó mucho.

¿Dónde te quedaste? – Me quedé en un hotel barato.

¿Qué hiciste el día del festival? – Llegué temprano al pueblo para coger sitio.

¿Cuál es una regla importante? – No se debe tirar piedras, solo tomates.

¿Cómo fue la batalla de tomates? – La batalla fue muy apasionante y divertida.

¿Qué hiciste después de la batalla? – Volví al hotel y me duché.

¿Qué tiempo hizo? – Hizo sol por la mañana, pero luego llovió.

¿Qué fue lo mejor del día? – Lo mejor fue tirar tomates a la gente.

¿Qué te pareció la experiencia? – Fue una experiencia inolvidable.

¿Te gustaría volver algún día? – Sí, me encantaría.

2. Sentence puzzle

a) Háblame de tu viaje a Buñol   b) ¿ Por qué decidiste ir a la Tomatina?   c) ¿ Cómo viajaste y cómo fue el viaje?

d) ¿ Qué hiciste el día del festival?   e) ¿ Qué tiempo hizo por la mañana?   f) ¿ A qué hora llegaste al pueblo?

g) ¿Qué hiciste por la tarde?   h) ¿ Qué fue lo mejor del día?   i) ¿ Qué te pareció la experiencia?

j) ¿ Te gustaría volver en el futuro?   k) ¿ Qué hiciste después de la batalla de tomates?

3. Guided translation

a) ¿Cuándo fuiste a Buñol? ¿Cómo viajaste?   b) ¿Con quién fuiste?   c) ¿Qué tiempo hizo por la mañana?

d) ¿Dónde te quedaste? ¿Te gustó?   e) ¿Cuál es una regla importante?   f) ¿Qué hiciste durante la batalle de tomates?

g) ¿Qué fue lo mejor del día?

4. Answer the following questions in your own words, using full sentences

Students own answer, based on language from this unit.

Vocab Revision Workout 7

1. Gapped translation

a) month   b) rented   c) nice/good   d) cheap   e) far   f) liked   g) young people

2. Verb anagrams

a) pasé   b) hizo   c) fuimos   d) alojamos   e) había   f) comieron   g) jugó   h) hicimos

3. Select the correct preterite form

a) hicieron   b) alquilé   c) limpió   d) salieron   e) vino   f) jugó   g) vimos   h) se levantó   i) me quedé

j) fuimos   k) estudiaron   l) comió   m) vinieron   n) leyó

4. Complete with any suitable verb

a) fue   b) hizo   c) vio   d) montó   e) jugó   f) relajó   g) levantó   h) sacó/tomó   i) fue   j) jugó   k) compró/llevó   l) leyó

m) viajó   n) escuchó

5. Match questions and answers

¿Adónde fuiste de vacaciones? – A Lloret de Mar, en la costa

¿Cuándo fuiste? – En agosto

¿Cómo viajaste? – Alquilamos un coche

¿Con quién fuiste? – Con mi familia

¿Dónde te alojaste? – En un hotel muy caro

¿Dónde estaba el hotel? – Estaba cerca de la playa, a orillas del mar

¿Cómo era el hotel? – Era lujoso, muy grande y moderno

¿Qué había en el hotel? – Una piscina muy grande, un gimnasio y tres restaurantes

¿Cuánto tiempo te quedaste allí? – Una semana

¿Cómo era tu habitación? – Era muy espaciosa y estaba bien cuidada

¿Qué había en tu habitación? – Una cama cómoda, un escritorio, un sofá y una televisión

6. Complete

a) Fui de vacaciones a Alemania   b) Viajé en autocar   c) Fui allí con mi familia   d) El viaje fue aburrido

e) No me gustó mucho el hotel   f) Lo pasamos muy bien   g) Nos alojamos en un albergue juvenil

h) Sin embargo, había mucho que hacer   i) Había una piscina y un gimnasio

7. Translate into Spanish

a) El primer día visitamos el museo   b) El segundo día alquilamos una bicicleta   c) El tercer día fueron de turismo

d) Por la mañana se levantó tarde   e) Tomé el sol en la playa hasta mediodía   f) Hicimos senderismo todos los días

g) Ayer dio un paseo / fue de paseo   h) Nadamos en el mar   i) Nos alojamos en un hotel barato

j) Por la noche mis padres fueron de marcha   k) Probaron muchos platos típicos

8. Translate into Spanish

El verano pasado, mi hermano mayor fue a España con su novia.

Se quedaron en un pueblo pequeño en la Costa Brava, a una hora de Barcelona.

Alquilaron una casa no lejos de la playa. (*accept*: cerca de)

La casa estaba limpia y era acogedora. Había una televisión, pero no había Internet.

La playa era bonita, así que pasaron todos los días allí tomando el sol, nadando, dando largos paseos por la orilla y viendo atardeceres.

Por la noche fueron a restaurantes y probaron platos típicos locales.

Lo mejor fue cuando hicieron buceo.

Unit 15: Talking about a day trip to Cádiz & Sevilla – past & future

1. Match

Había un castillo – There was a castle   **Es una ciudad histórica** – It's a historic city   **Está en la costa** – It's on the coast
El viajé duró – The journey lasted   **La gente era** – The people were   **Estaba en el centro** – It was in the centre
Nos alojamos – We stayed   **El viaje fue** – The journey was   **Me gustó** – I liked it   **Lo mejor fue** – The best thing was
Estaba limpio – It was clean   **Hizo buen tiempo** – The weather was nice   **Me gustaría volver** – I would like to go back

2. Complete the words

a) Un castillo b) Nos alojamos c) La gente d) El viaje e) Me gustó f) Acogedora g) Lo mejor

h) El tiempo i) Estaba limpio j) Un paseo k) El puerto

3. Break the flow

a) Hace dos días fui a Cádiz.   b) Cádiz es una ciudad histórica.   c) El viaje fue bastante largo.

d) El viaje duró casi una hora.   e) En Cádiz nos quedamos en un hotel.   f) La gente era muy amable.

g) El hotel estaba limpio.   h) Estaba muy cerca del puerto.   i) Hicimos muchas cosas.

4. Complete with the missing words

a) Hace dos **días** fuimos a Cádiz   b) El viaje duró dos **horas**   c) Cádiz es una **ciudad** histórica

d) Está situada en el **sur** de España   e) Viajamos en **coche**   f) Nos quedamos en un hotel **barato** cerca del centro

g) El hotel **estaba** limpio y el personal era amable y **acogedor**   h) Hizo buen **tiempo**   i) Visitamos la **catedral** y el **castillo**

j) Comimos **marisco** en un restaurante típico en el puerto   k) Alquilamos una bici y dimos una **vuelta** por el centro

l) Por la noche mi hermano mayor fue de **marcha**   m) Me gustaría **volver** a Cádiz el año próximo

5. Spot and correct the nonsense sentences

a) Cádiz es ~~un hotel histórico~~ **una ciudad histórica**   b) El viaje duró ~~un año.~~ **una hora**   c) –

d) Desafortunadamente hizo ~~buen~~ **mal** tiempo   e) Hicimos turismo en ~~mi habitación~~ **el centro / el casco antiguo**

f) Comimos marisco en ~~la catedral~~ **un restaurante / el puerto**

g) Alquilamos un ~~avión~~ **coche (o una bici)** y visitamos el casco antiguo h) -

6. Sentence puzzle

a) Hace una semana fui con mi familia a Cádiz b) El viaje fue bastante largo c) Pasamos dos días en Cádiz

d) Llegamos el sábado por la mañana e) Nos quedamos en un hotel muy bueno f) El hotel estaba cerca del centro

g) Visitamos una catedral muy grande   h) También fuimos a ver un castillo antiguo

i) Probamos muchos platos típicos de la región   j) Comimos marisco en un restaurante cerca del puerto

7. Gapped translation

a) **Last week** I went to Cadiz b) We travelled by **coach** It was very **slow**   c) We woke up **very early**

d) The journey was **long** and **tiring** e) We stayed in a **three star** hotel   f) The hotel was in the **port** of Santa María

g) We spent two **unforgettable days** h) We **ate** very tasty local **dishes** i) We visited a very **pretty/beautiful castle**

j) We did a bike tour of the **old** town k) The hotel staff was very **welcoming**

8. Translate into English

a) Last month b) I spent two unforgettable days c) We stayed in a youth hostel

d) It was near the beach, a 5 minute walk away e) We rented a bicycle and went sightseeing

f) We took many photos of old buildings g) The best (thing) was when we visited the castle h) I also loved the local food

i) We met welcoming and helpful people j) Fortunately, it was sunny every day

9. Guided translation

a) La semana pasada   b) Pasé tres días en Cádiz   c) Viajamos en autocar   d) Nos quedamos en un hotel barato

e) El hotel estaba cerca del puerto   f) Todos los días hicimos turismo   g) El último día alquilé una bici

h) Fuimos a ver la catedral   i) También visitamos el castillo   j) Cerca del museo

k) Conocimos a dos chicos muy simpáticos   l) Fuimos a la playa con ellos

10. Find the Spanish equivalent of the following in Parts 1 and 2 of Manolo's text

a) Está en la costa   b) Hay muchas cosas que hacer   c) Lo mejor es que   d) Viajamos   e) El viaje en autocar fue muy aburrido

f) Nos alojamos   g) La gente del hotel era muy amable

11. Complete the statements below based on the content of Parts 3 & 4

a) Every day Manolo woke up **early**   b) After breakfast he went **walking/for a walk** in town

c) One day he ate **seafood** in the port   d) It was the **best** he has had in his life   e) The water was **clean** but very **cold**

f) His parents didn't go to **the beach**   g) One day his parents visited a **castle** and the **next** day the Roman theatre

h) He thinks his parents are a bit **boring**

12. Tick the words/phrases contained in part 4 and cross out the ones that aren't

a) ~~However~~   b) **Always**   c) ~~Went for a walk~~   d) **On the last day**   e) **Boring**   f) ~~It was sunny~~   g) **To sunbathe**

h) **Beach**   i) ~~We called each other~~   j) **We write to each other**

13. Answer the following questions about Manolo's whole text

a) It is very far from Sitges.   b) In quite a cheap hotel, near the centre.   c) It was the best he's ever had in his life.

d) Because they went sightseeing (instead) every day.   e) Went the the beach / relaxed.   f) Intelligent, sporty, very funny.

g) Chat/talk and play volleyball.   h) They still write to each other / he would love to see her again.

14. Complete the table

Tomorrow – **Mañana**   El viaje dura – **The trip takes/lasts**   Vamos a viajar – **We are going to travel**   By car – **En coche**

En avión – **by plane**   Voy a alojarme – **I am going to stay**   We are going to stay – **Vamos a quedarnos**

Lo mejor será – **The best thing will be**   On the first day – **El primer día**   El segundo día – **On the second day**

Vamos a visitar – **We are going to visit**   Vamos a hacer turismo – **We are going to go sightseeing**

We are going to try – **Vamos a probar**   We are going to eat – **Vamos a comer**

15. Complete with a suitable word (accept any other correct suggestions)

a) ir/viajar   b) amigo/a/novio/a/familia   c) coche/barco/avión)   d) hotel/albergue   e) café/tostadas/cereales

f) bici/moto   g) lugares/monumentos   h) fotos   i)visitar/ver   j) comer   k) paseo   l) divertido/interesante/aburrido

16. Slalom translation

a) Vamos a pasar dos días en Sevilla   b) Es una ciudad histórica en el sur de España   c) Tal vez vamos a alquilar una bici

d) El hotel está cerca de la calle principal   e) El viaje dura más o menos una hora   f) Vamos a alojarnos en un hotel barato

g) Voy a dar un paseo por el casco antiguo   h) Mi hermano va a sacar muchas fotos

i) Voy a probar los platos típicos de la región   j) Creo que el viaje será apasionante

17. Multiple choice choose the correct translation

I am going to stay ; I am going to go out ; I am going to travel ; I am going to have fun ; I am going to rest ; I am going to try ; I am going to buy ; I am going to rent ; I am going to dance ; I am going to go

18. Complete with the correct option

a) **comer**   b) **dar**   c) **visitar**   d) **alquilar**   e) **comprar**   f) **hacer**   g) **alojarme**   h) **viajar**   i) **salir**   j) **mirar**

k) **sacar**   l) **pasear**

19. Complete the table

Viajé en coche – **Voy a viajar en coche**   Comí – Voy a comer   Me alojé en un hotel – **Voy a alojarme en un hotel**

¿Adónde fuiste? – ¿Adónde vas a ir?   ¿Qué hiciste? – ¿Qué vas a hacer?

Mi hermano fue de marcha – Mi hermano va a ir de marcha

Mi madre compró recuerdos – **Mi madre va a comprar recuerdos**   **Mi padre sacó fotos** – Mi padre va a sacar fotos

Mi hermano y yo compramos ropa – **Mi hermano y yo vamos a comprar ropa**   Tomamos el sol – Vamos a tomar el sol

Mis padres visitaron museos – **Mis padres van a visitar museos**

20. Answer the following questions about Parts 1 to 3 of Veronica's text

a) Greece (but originally from Barbastro) b) Her best friend c) Coach

d) The Spanish fast train – because it is as fast as a bird! e) A youth hostel in the city centre

f) Morning walk in the María Luisa park / Afternoon Ate tapas in a local restaurant

g) Morning went to the museum of fine arts / Afternoon nothing special / walk in town / rest in the hostel

h) A painter/artist i) Because they were tired

21. Complete the translation of Part 4

I loved the **trip/journey**. I **think** that Sevilla is my favourite **city** in Spain. Therefore, this year I am going to **return to** Sevilla again! Next **week** I am going to **travel** to Sevilla by **train** On the **first** day, in the morning, I am going to go for a **walk** in the old **town** and the **Triana** neighbourhood. After that I am going to **see** the Real Alcázar gardens. In the **evening** I am going to go out in the **town centre** and eat tapas in a very **well known** local restaurant.

22. Find the Spanish equivalent in the text

a) tan rápido como un pájaro b) solo dura c) un albergue juvenil d) muchas cosas e) (los) patos f) ricas g) del pintor

h) le gustó i) nada especial j) me encantó el viaje k) por lo tanto l) voy a volver m) el casco antiguo n) muy conocido

o) he visto fotos p) donde se puede comer q) tengo muchas ganas r) un espectáculo de flamenco

23. Complete the text below choosing from the options provided

Hola, me llamo Alejandro. **soy** de Gerona, en el norte de España, pero **vivo** en Italia. El año pasado **fui** de vacaciones a Granada, en el sur de España. **Viajé** con mi mejor amigo Marco. Granada **está** muy lejos de Gerona. **Viajamos** en tren desde Gerona hasta Zaragoza y luego **tomamos** el autocar hasta Granada. No me **gustó** nada el autocar. Me mareé *[I felt sick]* y tuve que vomitar en una bolsa de **papel**. El viaje en autocar de Zaragoza a Granada **duró** más o menos nueve horas.

25. Gapped translation

a) El año **pasado** fui de vacaciones **a** Sevilla. b) No me **gustó** viajar en **autocar**. c) … **pero** me **encantó** el tren.

d) El primer día **me desperté** temprano. e) **En** Sevilla también **hizo** buen **tiempo**. f) Solo **llovió** un **día**.

g) **Tomamos** el tren **hasta** Sevilla. h) Mis padres no **fueron** a la playa. i) Por la tarde, no **hicimos** casi **nada**.

j) Lo **mejor** fue el **marisco** en Cádiz. k) Un día **conocí** a una **chica** muy graciosa.

26. Translate into Spanish

a) El año pasado b) Fuimos de vacaciones c) A Cádiz d) En el sur de España e) Es una ciudad bonita f) En la costa

g) Viajamos h) En tren i) Alquilamos una bici j) Nos alojamos/quedamos k) En un hotel barato l) En un albergue juvenil

m) Estaba en el centro n) Cerca de la calle principal/peatonal o) Dimos un paseo p) Por el casco antiguo

27. Find the Spanish equivalent

a) Siempre hace sol b) Tomamos un autocar c) Se puede ver d) Las calles típicas e) El viaje duró f) Nos quedamos

g) Me encantaron los edificios antiguos h) Voy a viajar i) Una ciudad británica j) Uno de los mejores hoteles

k) Vamos a visitar l) Hay muchas cosas que hacer m) Sacar fotos del estrecho n) Hay una que se llama

28. Answer in English

a) It is always sunny and the weather is nice b) The people are friendy & nice, and the food is delicious

c) An old Roman bridge d) They canoed down the river with a guide e) Next year f) English and Spanish

g) Excellent sea views h) At a café called Sacarello's i) It is one of the oldest in Europe

j) Any of see monkeys, take photos of the straits, visit St Michael's cave, visit the beaches k) A beach

l) There is also one in Cadiz

THE LANGUAGE GYM

29. Translate the following into English

a) The south of the country   b) The best thing   c) Last month   d) We stayed   e) The old buildings

f) With false/fake windows   g) The people   h) They have excellent sea views   i) To go for a walk

j) It will be a very exciting trip

30. Spot and correct the mistakes with the verbs

a) Ayer ella **fue** de vacaciones a Sevilla   b) Mis padres **hicieron** excursiones cada día   c) -

d) Nosotros **vamos** a viajar en coche   e) Mis padres **alquilaron** una bici   f) Yo **di** un paseo por el centro

g) Mi madre **va** a comprar recuerdos   h) Yo **voy** a ir a la playa   i) -   j) Nosotros **fuimos** al casco antiguo

k) Mis hermanos lo **pasaron** bomba   l) Ella **va** a probar la comida local   m) Yo **saqué** muchas fotos   n) -

31. Complete with *yo, tú, él/ella, nosotros/as, vosotros/as* or *ellos/as* (any gender)

a) Nosotros/as   b) Tú   c) Ellos/as   d) Vosotros/as   e) Él/ella   f) Yo   g) Ellos/as   h) Yo   i) Tú   j) Él/ella   k) Nosotros/as

l) Ellos/as   m) Él/ella   n) Él/ella

32. Translate the following texts into Spanish

1. Me llamo Felipe y soy de Mérida, en el oeste de España. Normalmente voy de vacaciones a Santiago de Compostela, en el noroeste de España. Me gusta mucho, pero siempre llueve. El año pasado fui de vacaciones a Sevilla, en el sur de España, con mi mejor amigo Carlos. Carlos es muy alto y divertido. Fuimos a Sevilla en tren y nos alojamos en un albergue juvenil. En Sevilla dimos un paseo por el centro de la ciudad y compramos recuerdos. Un día vimos un espectáculo de flamenco. Fue un viaje emocionante y me encantaría volver.

2. Me llamo Jaime y soy de Valencia, en el este de España. Normalmente voy de vacaciones a Madrid, en el centro de España. Me gusta mucho porque la gente es muy simpática. El año pasado fui de vacaciones a Barcelona, en el noreste de España, con mi novia María. María es inteligente y trabajadora. Fuimos a Barcelona en autocar y nos alojamos en un hotel barato. Vimos el parque Güell y fuimos a la playa. Un día dimos un paseo por las Ramblas. Fue un viaje divertido y nos gustaría volver el año próximo.

3. Me llamo Carola y soy de Granada, en el sur de España. Normalmente voy de vacaciones a Portugal. Me gusta mucho porque hace buen tiempo y la comida es deliciosa. El año pasado fui de vacaciones a Bilbao, en el norte de España, con mi mejor amiga Ana. Ana es fuerte y muy amable. Fuimos a Bilbao en avión y nos alojamos en un hotel de lujo. Vimos el museo Guggenheim y también visitamos la catedral. Lo mejor fue la gente y la comida. Fue un viaje interesante y me gustaría volver algún día.

Question Skills Unit 15

1. Match questions and answers

¿Adónde fuiste? – A Cádiz, en el sur de España

¿Cómo viajaste? – En autocar

¿Cómo fue el viaje? – Fue muy largo y agotador

¿Dónde te alojaste? – En un albergue juvenil muy bueno

¿Qué viste? – Vi muchos monumentos y ruinas antiguas

¿Qué hiciste en Cádiz? – Hice turismo y visité monumentos

¿Qué sitios visitaste? – Visité un museo, un castillo y una catedral

¿Qué tiempo hizo? – Hizo sol todos los días

¿Qué fue lo que más te gustó de Cádiz? – Lo mejor fue la comida, por supuesto

¿Qué te pareció la gente?– La gente era muy acogedora y servicial

¿Te gustaría volver algún día? – Sí, me gustaría mucho

2. Sentence puzzle

a) ¿ Adónde fuiste de vacaciones el verano pasado?   b) ¿ Qué te pareció la gente de Sevilla?

c) ¿ Qué tiempo hizo durante las vacaciones?   d) ¿ Qué fue lo que más te gustó de la ciudad?

e) ¿ Por qué te gustaría volver allí?   f) ¿ Qué lugares históricos visitaste en Cádiz?   g) ¿ Qué hiciste por la tarde?

h) ¿ Qué vas a hacer el verano próximo?   i) ¿Con quién vas a viajar?

3. Guided translation

a) ¿Adónde fuiste el fin de semana pasado?   b) ¿Cómo viajaste?   c) ¿Con quién viajaste?   d) ¿Cuántos días te quedaste?

e) ¿Cómo fue el viaje?   f) ¿Dónde te alojaste?   g) ¿Qué hiciste por la tarde?   h) ¿Qué lugares visitate?   i) ¿Qué tiempo hizo?

j) ¿Qué fue lo que te gustó más?

4. Write a question for each of the answers below

a) ¿Cómo vas a viajar?   b) ¿Cuánto tiempo vas a quedarte?   c) ¿Qué tiempo hizo?

d) ¿Qué tal lo pasaste? / ¿Cómo lo pasaste?   e) ¿Qué (actividades) hiciste?   f) ¿Con quién fuiste?

g) ¿Qué hicieron tus padres?   h) ¿Qué viste?   i) ¿Dónde te alojaste?   j) ¿ Dónde estaba el hotel?

5. Spot and correct the mistakes in the Spanish sentences

a) ¿**Cuándo** fuiste a España?   b) ¿Con **quién** viajaste?   c) ¿Cómo **fue** el viaje?   d) ¿**Dónde** te alojaste?   e) ¿Qué sitios **visitó**?

f) ¿Por qué no te **gustó**?   g) ¿Qué **hicieron** por la tarde?   h) ¿Te gustaría **volver** allí?

6. Translate into Spanish

a) ¿Adónde fuiste?   b) ¿Con quién fuiste?   c) ¿Cuánto tiempo te quedaste (allí)?   d) ¿Dónde te alojaste?

e) ¿Cómo era el hotel?   f) ¿Qué hiciste por la mañana?   g) ¿Qué hiciste por la tarde?   h) ¿Qué hicieron tus padres?

i) ¿Te gustaría volver algún día?

THE LANGUAGE GYM

Printed in Great Britain
by Amazon

58155822R00044